132 WAYS
TO EARN A LIVING
WITHOUT
WORKING
(For Someone Else)

132 WAYS
TO EARN A LIVING
WITHOUT
WORKING
(For Someone Else)

Ed Rosenthal
& Ron Lichty

St. Martin's Press • New York

Designed by Laurel Marx

Library of Congress Cataloging in Publication Data

Rosenthal, Ed.
    132 ways to earn a living without working (for someone else)

    Includes bibliographies.
      1. Self-employed—Handbooks, manuals, etc.
2. Small business—Handbooks, manuals, etc.
I. Lichty, Ron, joint author.   II. Title.
HD8036.R67   658.1'141   78-19407
ISBN 0-312-40102-7
ISBN 0-312-40103-5 pbk.

The Cap'n he said to John Henry
I'm gonna bring that steam drill round
Gonna bring that steam drill out on the job
Gonna whop that steel on down, down, down.

John Henry, he said to his Cap'n
Cap'n, a man ain't nothin' but a man
But I would die die die with a hammer in my hand
Before I would let a steam drill beat me down.

John Henry, he hammered in the morning
He hammered all day long
He hammered so hard that he broke his poor heart
And he laid down his hammer and he died.

—*The Ballad of John Henry*

Learning is work. Caring for children is work. Community action is work. Once we accept the concept of work as something meaningful—not just as the source of a buck—you don't have to worry about finding enough jobs.

—*Ralph Helstein, President Emeritus,*
United Packinghouse Workers of America,
as quoted by Studs Terkel

You can get it if you really want,
You can get it if you really want,
You can get it if you really want,
But you must try,
Try and try,
Try and try, and
You'll succeed at last.

—*You Can Get It If You Really Want,*
SUNG BY JIMMY CLIFF

FOREWORD

This book is written for people who want to generate enough cash to live comfortably. It is not a get-rich-quick book. It is for people who do not have a high overhead and who understand that it is not only how much you make, but how you spend your money and your time, which determine quality of life.

People spend widely different amounts for products which perform the same function. For example, one can spend $200, $500 or $5000 for a car which can legally go no faster than 55 miles per hour. With a little bit of money, time and creativity I fixed up my $100 car, which was a very safe vehicle, re-upholstered it, and put in a used FM radio and stereo tape player. I logged 23,000 miles using off-brand gasoline. When the car broke down, I walked away from it with no sense of loss, something I couldn't have done if it had cost $5000. For that price I would have been constantly worried about theft, as well as scratches, dents and weird engine noises.

Buying used appliances and clothing really cuts the cost of living. So does growing your own food and buying the rest through food conspiracies (informal food co-ops which buy in bulk from wholesale distributors and divide it up among members).

Consumer products are a plot to keep people working. When you learn to buy really cheaply, make your own, or not amass so many possessions, you will find far less need to work.

I know people who pay $600 a month to live in a two-room

apartment in an expensive high-rise building. They are paying for status—which is the most expensive thing you can try to buy. In order to live there, they each have to pay $300 a month rent—two-thirds of my monthly budget. Yet I live better than they do—with frequent vacations, travel, plenty of good food and lots of entertainment.

Americans tend to equate living expensively with living well. This is not really true. People who labor at work they don't like are not living well no matter how much money they make. These people are wasting the most precious commodity they own—one they can't buy: time. Each person has only so much of it. Any use of it which isn't fulfilling and enjoyable is a waste.

PREFACE

There are hundreds of thousands of ways to make a living, and choosing the right method for you is probably the most important choice you'll ever make.

You *could* be a secretary, a machinist or a construction worker. There's nothing wrong with those jobs. But, personally, neither of us would care to do them for the rest of our lives. Those jobs sound too much like work, "work" being something you don't *enjoy*. Among the synonyms for "work" listed in *Webster's Dictionary of the English Language* are "grind" and "drudgery."

Making a living doesn't have to be work, drudgery or a grind. Thousands of people earn a living doing what they enjoy—and that's fun, not work.

The methods of earning a living described in this book are not to be found in any career guidance manual. Most guidance books attempt to make professionals who will join the corporate structure.

We're offering you an opportunity to stay human. We explain how to earn a living doing a part-time or full-time gig. The methods are untraditional. Some of them even impart a negative status (to some people; others feel admiration and envy for those who've found ways to live their lives creatively), they're so untraditional. But then, you can't eat status.

There are tens of thousands of ways to make a living without working for someone else. There are so many of them, in fact, that what we've done is to select 132 genres of workstyles, some that you may have heard of but not thought of recently, and others which are more unusual. We've tried to give you an idea of what they involve. We've dug out resources we think you'll find helpful in starting them up.

Use your creativity and originality to expand on the ideas here. Take the idea of becoming a street or party entertainer, for example. How about painting murals on the sides of buildings? Or being a recreational director on an ocean liner? Or a musician on a cross-country train? Or, in many cases, you can start an agency to do these jobs and employ both yourself and your friends.

Above all, do what you enjoy and be creative. If you enjoy baking, bake! A home-baked pie route can make a living for you, as it has for others.

One more thing. Imagine someone giving you this advice at your local career counseling office:

> Well, Fred, after looking at your career guidance test and interest sheet, it seems to me that with your interests and goals, you might want to become a marijuana farmer. The career has tremendous opportunities and with your personality and interest in botany, you should be able to build up quite a business.

Or how about this:

> Susan, from what you've told me about yourself, I think you have the potential to take on junk collecting in a big way. Judging from your knowledge of the dumpsters in the area and your keen desire to turn garbage into treasures, you should go far in the field.

You couldn't imagine it? Well, read on.

HOW TO USE THIS BOOK

You are probably reading this book because you are frustrated by your job. Although you may feel alone, the truth is, many Americans hate their work. They find their jobs boring and routine, offering them little satisfaction, little feeling of accomplishment, little fun.

Most likely you have said to yourself, "It would be great if I could earn a living at something I find interesting and like doing." You probably already have marketable skills. Use them creatively to become independent of the corporate structure.

The purpose of this book is to help spark your creativity. The 132 ways discussed in this book were chosen from thousands to show you what you can do if you use your ingenuity. All of these ways are working for people right now. One of them could work for you. Or your idea, the one that's been simmering on the back burner of your creative mind, might be even better.

There are many questions to ask before starting any new venture:

Will I enjoy starting this business?
Will I enjoy keeping it running?
Does it fit in with my personal short- and long-term goals?
Is the proposal a sound business idea?
Can it work where I am living?
How much money can I expect to make from it?
Am I willing to put in the time to run it?

Is it a long-term project?
Am I willing to commit myself for that long?
Do I have access to the capital needed to start it?
How long will I have to wait before I see the first profits?
Do I have money to live on while I am waiting for the first
    profits?

You should also find out what kinds of licenses, business certificates and permits are required to operate in your area.

Your answers to these questions will help you to decide what situation is best for you. Remember that each situation is unique and different from all others; there is no magic formula.

Most of these ideas can be begun in your spare time. That gives you a chance to try out your fantasy, and determine whether it will make you money—and whether you can be happy doing it for a living.

Perhaps you would enjoy doing several different things for a living. For instance, you could sell crafts occasionally, run a small plant nursery, and cut firewood. Variety is the spice of life. Routine destroys creativity and sensitivity. Things that are fun once a week become boring once a day.

Sometimes you'll find that things that do not provide a living pay very handsomely by providing for your personal needs. You can grow food, gather firewood, make clothing and salvage furniture. Every time you perform a service for yourself, you don't have to work to pay for that service. You eliminate the middleperson's markup and taxes, and you make yourself a little more independent.

PART I
BEING
WITH PEOPLE

1
BOARDING HOUSE/ ROOMING HOUSE

Louis Jordan had been a union carpenter. He worked in construction eight months a year, and did freelance repair work on weekends and during the winter. Mrs. Jordan had graduated from high school and married a year later. The only job she had ever held was clerk in a local drugstore when she was 17. After 25 years of marriage, and raising four children, she and her husband had looked forward to the security that a lifetime of hard work deserved.

Susan Jordan's husband died one month after their youngest child, Rachel, graduated from college. Now Rachel was living away from home, Mrs. Jordan was all alone in her seven-room San Francisco Victorian flat. (The upstairs flat had always been rented out; it just about paid all the expenses of ownership—taxes, insurance, upkeep and repair.) Her husband's pension "would take care of her," but for the first time, she "had to face life alone."

Her only skill was housekeeping. She liked the routine of shopping, cooking and light housekeeping. She placed an ad in the daily classifieds, "Live in my house, share food, rent and companionship. I have room for three refined, middle-aged, single people." Within the week, the three extra bedrooms were rented to Susan's new "family"—a woman and two men.

Her "family" depends on her for meals and light housekeeping and each is happy to pay $240 a month for room and board. They have been together for over two years. "We have grown very attached to each other," says Susan.

Michael Smith lives in a large five-bedroom house in the Berkeley foothills. He leases the entire house and lets rooms to his friends. He divides the rent and utilities four ways and lives rent-free. In return, he handles all the problems and chores of dealing with the landlord and utility companies.

Two years ago, Larry Harmond bought an old dormitory frat house. He painted and refinished it, and rents out rooms with kitchen privileges to students. "I take out only what I need to live on. I use the rest to pay off the mortgage." He says that he spends about ten hours a week on repair and upkeep. "The hardest part of this whole deal was the mortgage." He had to borrow from relatives and friends to make the down payment.

Susan, Michael and Larry have all found a living (or part of one) in running boarding and rooming houses. They share many qualities: commitment, a deep sense of responsibility, and satisfaction in keeping a structure functioning. They feel comfortable living with roommates, and they enjoy sharing space with other people.

To start you need a house, or enough capital to lease or buy one, and some practical how-to knowledge of house repair. You can advertise for roomers in local papers, church, club or school journals, on bulletin boards, and by word of mouth. It is crucial to select the right people; you will be living close to them, so make sure everyone is compatible. There are no fixed rules for how a house is run. Each situation calls for a different structure, depending on the people and circumstances.

OTHER IDEAS:

In Miami, Cindy Johnson and Jerri Jenkins started Home-at-Last, Inc., to provide a homelike atmosphere for traveling celebrities.

In San Francisco, Robert Pritikin bought a large Victorian house and redecorated it in "the ambience of the turn of the century." "The Mansion," now a hotel, is booked up three months in advance by guests wanting to avoid the monotony of large hotels.

Three bachelors in Pittsburgh share meals in their dining room with several paying guests. Meals are served six days a week; guests and house members each cook and clean up once a week. They say that it is a great way to meet eligible women, cuts kitchen time in half, and actually makes a little money.

TO FIND OUT MORE:

Landlording: A Handymanual for Scrupulous Landlords Who Do It Themselves (by Leigh Robinson Express, Box 1373, Richmond, CA 94802, 1977) is a landlord's own book on how-to, maintenance, repairs, getting good tenants, rents, evictions, records, taxes, insurance and security. Packed with information.

2
BABYSITTER

If you care about and enjoy playing with kids and feel comfortable being responsible for them, babysitting may be a good way to earn a living for you.

The common image of a babysitter is of a high-school girl who gets a dollar or two per hour for sitting with a neighbor's kids for an evening. You can do more.

Some people sit with preschool children of working parents every working day. You can sit in the parents' homes or yours. Families sometimes offer free rent and board in partial payment, making you a live-in sitter. Upper-class families frequently hire nannies to supervise toddlers, young children, and sometimes teenagers.

Some parents expect you only to watch the kids. Others look for someone with an educational background who will see to it that the kids are challenged to think in their play.

To find kids to watch, tell friends and relatives you're available; advertise in women's centers, on bulletin boards or in classifieds. You'll probably need references to persuade strangers to trust you with their children. References from relatives, friends and/or neighbors should be enough.

OTHER IDEAS:

If you're watching kids in your home, you might want to watch kids from several families, setting up your own day-care center or children's nursery (check local licensing laws).

Take older children on afternoon trips, to museums or events or on weekend outings. Parents will be glad to pay to keep their children occupied.

Some teachers run summer camps and academies.

Run a babysitter service, placing sitters with families.

Run a babysitter switchboard connecting mothers to share sitting.

TO FIND OUT MORE:

The U.S. Office of Child Development (Dept. of Health, Education and Welfare, Washington, DC 20201) publishes many materials on kids, including "Infant Care," "Day Care for Your Children," "The Pocket Guide to Babysitting," and a long series on child-care/day-care centers. Request a catalog. (One of the day-care books, for example, focuses on serving children with special needs and has invaluable information in this area.)

The National Association for the Education of Young Children (1834 Connecticut Ave., N.W., Washington, DC 20009) is a nonprofit association of nearly 23,000 members and 150 affiliate groups which publishes the bimonthly journal *Young Children* (also available by subscription). If you're thinking of opening a care center, send for the free brochure, "The Essentials for Developing a Good Early Childhood Program," which offers valuable advice.

The Child Welfare League of America, Inc. (67 Irving Place, New York, NY 10003) is a membership association which makes available a series of selected bibliographies on: Day Care Costs; Day Care for Migrant Family Children; Group Day Care of Infants and Very Young Children; Parent Participation and Education in Day Care; and a general bibliography on Day Care Services (send a stamped, self-addressed envelope). It publishes a monthly journal, *Child Welfare*, and a bimonthly newsletter as well as many books in the field (catalog available free), such as *Guide for Establishing and Operating Day Care Centers for Young Children.*

Metropolitan Life Insurance Company (Health and Welfare Division, 1 Madison Ave., New York, NY 10010, or order from a local district office) publishes a card—"First Aid for the Family"—and two booklets—"Sitting Safely for Baby Sitters" and "Day Care—What & Why"—for folks in the child-care field. All are free.

Day Care: How to Plan, Develop, and Operate a Day Care Center (by E. Belle Evans, Beth Shub, Marlene Weinstein, Beacon Press, 1971) is a complete guide to day care, rules and regulations, teachers, health, play, classrooms and finances.

Day Care for Infants (by E. Belle Evans and George E. Saia, Beacon Press, 1972) provides an excellent guide to setting up, funding and running day care for infants and toddlers under age three.

The Day Care Book: The Why, What & How of Community Day Care (compiled by Vicki Breitbart, Alfred A. Knopf, 1974) is pro community day care, and advises on how to set up a center.

When Teenagers Take Care of Children (Public Health Service Publication #409-1964, Supt. of Documents, Washington, DC 20402) is a booklet on how to play with and care for children of various ages.

A Manual for Baby-Sitters (by Marion Lowndes, Little, Brown, 1975) lists 12 essentials for the babysitter to follow; it's worth its price for those four pages alone. It also discusses children of various ages and how to keep them happy and safe.

Day Nurseries for Preschoolers (Small Business Reporter, Bank of America NT & SA, San Francisco, CA 94120) is an eight-page how-to booklet of the basics.

3

LIMOUSINE SERVICE

Ronnie Sunshine runs a limo service in New York City that caters to young people and rock musicians. His first limousine had no windshield and looked downright funky, but he transported friends, their friends, and a number of rock groups, movie people, and artists. He solicited business outside the New York rock club Max's Kansas City. He made friends of recording company people. He hung out. He had fun. And he was always, it seemed, where the action was.

Other limousine services offer special rates to take you and your lover out for a night on the town, to give you a ride into town from the airport, for weddings, for funerals, for parties ("Imagine your guests' surprise when a limo pulls up in front of their door to bring them to your party"), and for business functions.

You need a special driver's license, insurance, and other permits. Check state and local laws.

OTHER IDEAS:

Run a long-distance limousine service which transports people to and from airports, the country, or special events.

Run a taxi-limousine switchboard, contacting drivers to respond to calls with their own vehicles.

4
MATCHING/
CONNECTING PEOPLE

Helping people find people—that's the name of the game in America's cities today. Ride services, travel partner services, dating services, roommate services—all are businesses set up to help people find each other.

Mimeographed or typed cards advertising ride services can be found on Laundromat, store and college bulletin boards all over the country. Call the listed number and the service will try to line you up with a ride for wherever you want to go. In most places there's room for at least one more good service. And all you need to get started is a telephone and some note cards.

If you're successful in finding rides for people, charge them a buck, or three, or five. Even with higher gas prices, auto travel is cheaper than the bus, the train or the plane. And it's even cheaper if you share the costs. Many ride services charge one fee to the person looking for a ride and another, lower fee to the person with the vehicle ($5 for the rider and $3 for the vehicle owner, for example).

The concept can be extended to travel partners. Single people are at a disadvantage traveling by themselves. Traveling in pairs can cut costs by as much as half, and at the same time double protection and increase entertainment possibilities. In New York, Travel Match charges an annual fee (with a guarantee) to match women up as travel partners; Francine Cohen, business owner, uses questionnaires as a basis for pairing.

Some of the people who use Travel Match are really looking for a new set of friends, acquaintances and associates which the other person can provide. Absurd as it seems, going through an agency is the only way thousands of people can find friends. This happens more often in cities than in small towns, but it really is a problem for people everywhere. Dozens of pen-pal agencies will link you up with a person in another country—or even in this country. And some pen-pal organizations will link you with someone of similar interests.

MENSA, the high-IQ society, has as one of its goals helping people with high intelligence find each other. It's nonprofit. But newsletters and newspapers and magazines are also published with the express purpose of helping people meet, and they make money at it.

Of course, many of the people looking for friends are specifically looking for friends of the opposite sex—to date or to do kinkier things with. *The Berkeley Barb* and the *Los Angeles Free Press* have thrived for years largely from sex-partner advertising. So do newsletters which circulate among nudists, gays and groupers.

On the other end of things, there are also newsletters designed solely to introduce people to each other for purposes of simple friendship or dating. And there are dating services. Again, they utilize questionnaires to match up pairs (sometimes matching is done by computers, other times by humans). If you find your dating service is underused by one sex, offer members of that sex lower rates.

A lot of single people are into living cheaply. And they know that doubling or tripling up in apartments can be less expensive and a lot more fun than living alone. Rooming together has become a necessity for many, especially with the rents being asked for apartments nowadays. College bulletin boards are lined with listings of people looking for roommates or communards. The more prudent, however, prefer to have potential roommates pre-screened. That's where a roommate service comes in. Matching people serves a real need. Mamselle in Manhattan, for example, matches women; it charges $40 to those looking for apartments and roommates, and $25 to those who have an apartment to share. Each customer is interviewed and fills out an extensive questionnaire. The Berkeley Connection matches people by lifestyle. It lists apartment-holders looking for roommates and charges apartment-seekers for its referrals.

There is even a Rent-A-Granny service in Albuquerque, New Mexico—it's an employment agency for the elderly and retired. In many cases, people are looking for surrogate grandparents to sit for their kids. The child and the surrogate grandparent often develop a relationship that distance prevents between the child and real grandparents.

For that matter, you could start a dating service, roommate service, or travel partner service geared solely to the elderly— they have the same wants and needs as everyone else.

OTHER IDEAS:

Jim Boulden, an entrepreneur from San Jose, modified the women's group/men's group concept. He sets up people's groups, which he calls "Interpersonal Support Networks," that meet in members' homes. Boulden charges each of the 15 people per group $20 per session; his only overhead is the salary of a "facilitator."

A desperate mother in Salt Lake City, Utah, set up a baby-sitting exchange service which charges a bimonthly registration fee and screens the potential member mothers.

In several large cities there are commercial musicians' and actors' switchboards which link performers with bands and orchestras and sometimes with clubs and other establishments looking for new talent.

In the San Francisco Bay area, the state government runs a computerized experimental carpool service for commuters. In other communities, individuals earn their livings providing this essential service for a small fee.

5
PIE KILL

Pie Kill was the brainstorm of two New York writers/lovers who decided to offer their fellow New Yorkers a pie in the face for only $40; a squirtgun barrage for $30; or a seltzer-water attack for $20. The client signed a contract on his or her victim, assuming full responsibility. And an agent of Pie Kill would be dispatched to do the deed. For an extra $10, a photograph of the attack would be taken before the agent made his or her escape.

Pie Kill received immediate publicity, and similar agencies

were started in other cities. Aron Kay, agent 008 of the original Pie Kill, pulls jobs regularly, specializing in conservative political figures.

Other outrageous ideas have attracted bucks from willing clients. A brother and sister in Tucson run an agency called Speak Easy, which for five to six dollars will telephone your anonymous message to the person you select. Clients tell off their bosses and break off relationships via the service. Speak Easy also passes on an occasional love message. In Philadelphia, Chutzpah Phone Service provides the same service and criticizes mothers-in-law, prods former husbands for alimony, and tells off barking-dog owners.

A San Franciscan started the Western Onion service, offering singing telegrams: original songs for 30 occasions. He charges $10 for phone delivery and $20 for personal delivery by bellhop-clad lads. He advertises two numbers—one a recorded demonstration tape, the other to place an order.

OTHER IDEAS:

Be a mercenary serenader, cheerleader, or chorus member.

6
PROSTITUTE

Prostitution is, for the most part, illegal. It is also a billion-dollar industry and one of the oldest businesses known, but it is not for everyone—many prostitutes develop psychological problems.

Most prostitutes are women who sell their bodies and sexual skills to men, although there are a growing number of male prostitutes who offer themselves to both men and women.

If you intend to solicit the opposite sex, probably the easiest way to get started is to find a member of that sex to help you— a friend, relative or former lover may help, either free or for a commission.

If there's a sex tabloid in your town, you could advertise there. Prostitutes on both coasts are soliciting customers (often truckers) via citizens band radio.

Or get to know a prostitute already in the trade and learn the business from him or her.

One of San Francisco's top hookers told the San Francisco *Chronicle* that her secret of success lies in sound business principles. "It's not that I'm better-looking or a better lay or anything else. There's no reason why anybody who had any kind of a brain in San Francisco couldn't make at least fifty thousand a year if they were diligent. I make way more."

Avoid hustling on street corners until you know the scene— you'll quickly run into problems, from either cops, pimps who feel they already have a claim on the territory, or bums.

Be careful. Be clean and get regular checks for the various venereal diseases. Be discreet.

OTHER IDEAS:

Specialize in a sex practice you enjoy, such as leather, whips and chains; sado-masochism; or dominance-submission.

7
FORTUNE TELLER/
ASTROLOGER/
DREAM INTERPRETER

Greek and Roman priests claimed to divine the future by observing the internal organs of sacrificial animals. Their prognoses may have altered plans of battles that ultimately shaped the fate of the world. Three thousand years later, fortune telling is still alive and well.

A Berkeley man claims he can tell anyone's fortune merely by looking deeply into their eyes; when he's found a victim, he looks deeply and says, "I can see you're involved in a relationship which is less than satisfying." He says the line is a perfect opening, since almost everyone is involved in at least one relationship which isn't satisfying. He doesn't claim to know the future, but claims anyone can read the present by using such universal statements.

Can people really tell you something about yourself with a crystal ball, the stars, your dreams, your palm, the Tarot, your tea leaves or the sediment in the bottom of your toilet bowl? Enough Americans believe so to support thousands of fortune tellers, astrologers and dream interpreters. There are even computer services which will compute an astrological report on you when you send in your check with your exact birth time and date.

TO FIND OUT MORE:

Fun in a Teacup: Your Complete Guide to Tea Leaf Reading (by Ian McKinnie, Celestial Arts, 231 Adrian Rd., Millbrae, CA 94030, 1974) is a complete guidebook to tea-telling.

The Encyclopedia of Ancient and Forbidden Knowledge (by Zolar, Nash Publishing, 9255 Sunset Blvd., Los Angeles, CA 90069, 1970) gives a broad overview of such occult sciences as astrology, Tarot, and numerology, as well as being a reference source.

The Modern Textbook of Astrology (by Margaret E. Hone) comes recommended by a number of astrologers as a helpful guide for the beginning astrologer.

There are thousands more books on astrology. And there are hundreds of books on dream analysis.

═══════════════ 8 ═══════════════

PERSONALIZE MATCHBOOKS

People love to see their names in print—especially when it's printed on something they can give to someone else. Most people, from teenagers to senior citizens, would be delighted to own boxes of personalized matchbooks or rolling papers to use and to give away. You can do the personalizing and make a living doing it.

The same machine will print lines of type onto matchbooks, business cards, or rolling-paper packs. The machine comes with hundreds of pieces of moveable type. You simply set the type to spell out each person's name or company's logo. Then, one by one, insert the matchbooks or rolling papers and stamp on the message.

Charge 50¢ or $1 for the first pack—setting the type takes the most time. Once it's set, you can whip out multiple copies in less time, so charge less for quantity.

Provide while-you-wait service on a street corner, at trade shows, in flea markets, at fairs and amusement parks, at parties or at schools.

While you've got people's attention, sell them picture buttons, letterheads or printed business cards. Machines are available which will wrap a Polaroid picture—or just about anything else —around a button.

You could make up posterboard backdrops with "For President," "Idiot of the Year," "Rolling Stoned," whatever, lettered on the posterboard to form a halo over your subject's head. Have your subject stand in front of the posterboard and take a picture with a Polaroid camera. Voilà! A personal campaign button in three minutes for $2.

Start your own print shop, or contract with an existing shop to print stationery items. You should be able to get reduced rates in return for bringing your wholesale business to a particular shop. Figure in a reasonable profit for yourself. And offer personalized stationery to your customers, to be mailed or delivered when ready. If you work with a quick-copy print shop, you may be able to take orders in the morning and deliver them in the afternoon.

Whatever you're personalizing, there's a huge market for your product. Market it properly and creatively, and you'll make a good living from the very thing people love most—their own names.

OTHER IDEAS: *No good with cigarette vending machine*

Personalized bumper stickers can also be a good seller. Some folks in Los Angeles sell them at local flea markets. During the "I Found It" campaign (a Madison Avenue-styled evangelistic crusade), lines of people waited to buy "I Lost It," "I Sold It" and "I Stepped in It" bumper stickers.

Frank Hadfield, a Cupertino, California, resident, sells personalized baseball cards printed with a picture of your personal hero. Little League ballplayers and junior-high students are depicted most often. The cards also list the young players' vital statistics.

Personalize newspaper headlines, T-shirts, belts and buckles, clothing, planters, jewelry, stash and jewelry boxes, bookplates, bookmarks, ceramics and dishes, trophies, drinking glasses (especially wedding reception champagne glasses), lunchboxes, car trinkets, balloons, key holders and wallets . . . the list is endless.

TO FIND OUT MORE:

Monarch Match Co. (2300 S. First St., San Jose, CA 95150) would love to set you up in business selling advertising book matches. They have a catalog filled with styles. They also sell an electric book match imprinter for about $200.

Badge-A-Minit (Box 618, Civic Industrial Park, LaSalle, IL 61301) is one of many badge- and personalized button-making systems (recent price under $40).

⑨
MASSEUR/MASSEUSE

Massage, as many have found, is an art of giving pleasure; and many of us find pleasure in giving it. If you're good at kneading muscles until they relax, and if you enjoy giving others the pleasure of relaxation, you may want to become a masseur or masseuse.

Massage is a skill, and there are many schools and teachers, and a wide variety of well-written how-to guides on the subject; you'll also be well massaged as part of your training. The most strenuous types of massage incude Shiatzu (Japanese), Rolfing (developed by Ida Rolf at Esalen Institute), and Polarity, which claims to enhance the body's energy flows. Each of these techniques is used to loosen the body and to increase body awareness. In addition to these nonsexual massages, there are many massage parlors which have a sexual orientation.

Most states now require training, testing or licensing for masseurs and masseuses.

Advertise your service like any other—on bulletin boards and in classifieds. Make it clear whether you're offering sexual or nonsexual massage.

A chiropractic student in Illinois contracted with a YMCA to run a massage service in the Y's Businessmen's Club.

OTHER IDEAS:

Run a massage workshop for couples. Advertise it "for lovers and friends."

Run a massage service or shop. Emphasize that your employees (co-workers) are trained and licensed professionals.

Offer your service at commercial hot-tub, steambath or sauna studios.

10

AGENT

Being an agent takes chutzpah and hustle, and can be very rewarding financially.

You can be a literary agent, a show business agent, or a music agent. Each usually begins by finding artists, established or aspiring, and then linking their work with the people who will produce it.

A literary agent in Berkeley, California, for example, is building a "stable" of the best writers he can find in the Berkeley area. He holds weekly writing workshops for them where they read what they're working on, exchange ideas and criticism with their peers, and get impetus to continue producing.

The agent attempts to market their work; he tries the top markets first, since he gets a 10 percent commission on the sale of each article, script, poem or book. He says when he first became a literary agent, he expected it to be difficult to get to the editors who buy manuscripts. He says he's found it quite easy to meet and talk with and sell to editors. The hard part, he says, has been keeping his writers working; most of them, it seems, are annoyingly laid-back.

The agent must be proficient in a number of areas. He or she must be able to keep the artists both using and improving their skills. The agent may provide some kind of subsistence-level work for starving artists (one offers work writing pornography and articles for several small area weeklies). Most important, the agent must be able to judge the salability of the various artists, to visualize markets for them, and to sell those markets hard.

OTHER IDEAS:

Open a lecture agency, supplying speakers to women's groups, men's organizations, and civic and fraternal groups.

Start a booking agency for small local bands.

Rep local artists to major market galleries.

A New York talent agency represents animals used for stage and screen events, parties and publicity.

TO FIND OUT MORE:

The Society of Authors' Representatives, Inc. (101 Park Ave., New York, NY 10017) has available a pamphlet titled "The Literary Agent" which is helpful in detailing what an agent can (and can't) do, standard practice of agents, and how writers find and contact agents. A self-addressed, stamped envelope must accompany requests for this pamphlet.

START A RELIGION/ PREACHER/MINISTER

In 1976, attention was drawn to the Universal Life Church and to the privileges afforded ministers when, to protest astronomical property taxes, 70 percent of the population of an upstate

New York town became Universal Life Church ministers on the same day. All were sworn in. All declared their property as religious property—nontaxable under the First Amendment to the Constitution as it has been interpreted for 200 years.

Even more savings can be realized when you charter your church (it takes three persons—pastor, secretary and treasurer) and vote your home to be church headquarters. You can not only save up to 50 percent on your federal income taxes (savings on state income taxes vary from state to state), but your church can pay the mortgage or rent as your pastor's "housing allowance," utility bills, medical care costs, travel expenses, a pastor's "clothing allowance," and home (church) furnishings.

The Internal Revenue Service Code requires your church to have the three officers, three members (who may be the same as the officers), a statement of beliefs or doctrine, and regular religious meetings (once a month is adequate) where some sacrament or ritual is performed.

Nationwide church organizations which license local churches include the Universal Life Church (Modesto, California), the Mother Earth Church (Sacramento, California), and the Life Science Church (San Diego, California). Becoming a minister or a preacher is a fairly simple matter, since these church organizations will grant you your license to preach and to form a church inexpensively for a few dollars sent through the mail.

Ministers can make a great deal of money if they service the needs of their flocks. Reverend Ike preaches that the "root of all evil is not money, but the lack of money." He offers his parishioners, in return for donations, a blessing program to help them attain wealth with positive thought. When the basket is sent around in his church he says that he doesn't want to hear any change jingling.

Billy Graham has all his expenses paid by various church organizations, which own the house in which he lives and the islands on which he vacations.

Starting your own religion can be even more profitable, but also takes a great deal more chutzpah. Each state has corporate laws and requirements for starting a church. Art Kleps did it in the 1960's by writing the Boohoo Bible and offering to grant the title of Boohoo to others.

Reverend Moon started a religion with the precept that Jesus failed and died in vain. Instead, Reverend Moon says he is the new savior of mankind. He has thousands of followers who work for his organization but whose only pay consists of free room and board. These people solicit and beg money and run various businesses, from kosher-style delis to janitorial services. Because of the low overhead, profits, donations and contributions have made Moon a very rich man.

Maharaj Ji, an Indian accused of diamond smuggling, made headlines as a new guru in the early '70's. His organization was expanding quickly until a crusade meeting held in Dallas flopped. Although his followers are now few, he still leads a comfortable life.

12
START AN ORGANIZATION

The United States is a nation of groups. People form organizations based on common interests, professions, work, politics, religious belief, weight, social involvement, recreational interests, travel, consumerism, hobbies, sports, age, name, race, ethnic background, social status, intelligence, disease research—almost anything you can think of. There are associations, clubs, committees, companies, corporations, fraternities, groups, leagues, organizations and societies.

Whatever your interests, there are probably other people who have a common interest and would like to communicate with you. You can form a local organization with meetings, or a state or national one in which members correspond. Many, if not most, are small, informal groups—others are larger and are incorporated and chartered as nonprofit organizations. For example, my grandfather helped form a burial society with other immigrants from his native town.

To attract potential members, you may be able to get free air time (community announcements) on local radio and TV, and you may be able to appear on talk shows. Some newspapers carry "club news," and the local paper might be interested in doing a feature story on your project. Magazines and newsletters which specialize in your field can usually be counted on for free publicity. Bulletin boards everywhere can be used to attract members. For instance, post a notice for your aviation club at private airports.

Three people are enough to start an organization. If your programs are attractive, more will join. Larger clubs can offer members benefits other than the original purpose of membership—insurance, charter flights, group trips, group discounts, and discounts at stores and restaurants.

Organizations get their revenue from membership fees, donations, contributions, benefit shows, bazaars, garage sales, cake sales, car washes, civic and government programs, and fees for services.

Most organizations are nonprofit, although some do have stockholders (for example, Weight Watchers) and earn a profit. Most have limited budgets and are staffed voluntarily. Others pay their officers a salary. Frequently the founders are paid employees, doing the mundane work of stuffing envelopes, composing and printing newsletters, or planning group activities. Larger organizations may have a paid board of directors, an executive staff and a secretarian unit. (The Muscular Dystrophy Association and the American Automobile Association are good examples of nonprofits with large paid staffs).

Starting an organization is a good way to be involved in a

field in which you are interested, to meet other people with similar interests, and to earn a living at the same time.

OTHER IDEAS:

Start a consumer organization. California Cash Card offers members discounts at various stores for paying cash. The stores join because the owners prefer to deal in cash rather than credit and for the free publicity. Cash Card carriers pay a yearly membership fee.

TO FIND OUT MORE:

The True Believer: Thoughts on the Nature of Mass Movement (by Eric Hoffer, Mentor/NAL, 1966) is probably the most successful attempt at debunking mass movements yet written. It should provide some real insights into mass movements, their appeal, the people who join them and the psychology involved.

===============13===============
PRODUCE AND
PROMOTE PERFORMANCES

Concerts, plays, fights, musical revues, poetry readings, dance recitals, lectures and religious gatherings are all performances which someone produces and promotes. That someone can be you.

Bill Graham, nationally known rock impresario, began his career as business manager of the San Francisco Mime Troupe, then threw the first Acid Tests with Ken Kesey. He built his skills for producing, promoting and organizing into a major rock concert production business.

Producing large concerts involves: renting halls; organizing a small army of assistants and workers to cover security, lights, stage construction, sound, tickets, and legal hassles; keeping the police and the local community people happy; promotion; and risking money hiring bands whose popularity may be questionable.

Small concerts, on the other hand, are much simpler to produce. You have to perform the same functions, but on a smaller scale. Small halls might include church basements and coffeehouses rather than theaters and arenas.

A few years ago, a promoter in Lombard, Illinois, brought local bands from the Chicago area into a church coffeehouse. He made an agreement with each band to split the door receipts. The coffeehouse made its money on snacks and a subsidy from the local church. He helped the bands by providing them with a new hall to play. The neighborhood kids flocked in on Friday and Saturday evenings for the fun of it. He made enough doing it to pay his living expenses.

TO FIND OUT MORE:

Creative Book Company (P.O. Box 214998, Sacramento, CA 95821) publishes two books of interest to event producers: *Starting and Staging a Successful Community Arts Festival* and *How to Produce a Successful Theatre Festival*. Each will stimulate your creativity. Each covers fairly well all the aspects of producing festivals.

Campus Attractions (annual; Billboard, 9000 Sunset Blvd., Los Angeles, CA 90069) lists popular artists, promoters, other attractions such as comedy, magic, hypnotism and mime, and a concert-planning checklist.

═══ I4 ═══
TRAVEL AGENCY/
TOUR ARRANGER

Americans love to travel, and you can earn a living fulfilling their nomadic fantasies.

Start with the proposition that every interest group needs a tour. And start with your own interests. A group of Pennsylvania pot smokers did just that and organized tours of Colombia and other major marijuana-producing countries.

Or open a travel agency. Customers pay you the same fee they'd pay the airline for an airplane ticket—but when they pay you, you get to keep a commission.

Arranging tours means setting up transportation, lodging, and excursion trips for groups, and selling these tours to people.

Good-Travel Tours in Oakland, California, specializes in travel to the "real" South Pacific: their unusual tours have group members staying with villagers and experiencing village life and culture. Their maximum tour group size is 20.

Travel agencies must convince people that they can help fulfill clients' fantasies, save them money, and get them where they want to go with the least hassle.

OTHER IDEAS:

Set up an agency which lists families who will take in students and other visitors for short and long stays. Houseguests find staying with locals often gives them personal insights into the areas they're visiting and is usually much cheaper than hoteling it, as well. Your agency can do the initial matchmaking between hosts and visitors.

Set up an agency to put city dwellers onto farms for vacations and vice versa.

Set up tours for people on special diets. An agency in New York City has been specializing in kosher tours of Mexico for over 20 years.

Set up tours for organizations or affinity groups. One tour might be "A Plumber's Guide to London."

Wilderness Travel, Inc., conducts trips graded as leisure, moderate or strenuous. They range from nature walks through Baja California to a month-long climb up Mount Everest.

Mark Travel Service offers all-gay cruises using come-ons such as "We'd like to make your trip a ball."

Elizabeth Zierer, founder of Education Continentale, specializes in counseling parents about European schools and colleges.

TO FIND OUT MORE:

A dozen Ohio farm families have formed the Ohio Farm and Rural Vacation Association (brochure from Mrs. Kenny Johnson, Secretary, R.D. 1, Zanesfield, OH 43360). Your agency could send people their way. Or organize such an association in your area and fill an empty farmhouse or farm trailer.

The Organic Traveler (by Maxine W. Davis and Gregory J. Tetralt, Grasshopper Press, Diamond Lake Station, P.O. Box 19053, Minneapolis, MN 55419, 1975)—if you're helping people plan their travels, be aware of books like this one, which you can certainly sell from your agency office—it's a state-by-state, city-by-city guide to health-food restaurants.

Touring with Towser: A Directory of Hotels and Motels that Accommodate Guests with Dogs (Gaines Dog Research Center, 250 North St., White Plains, NY 10625, 1971): You'll be much appreciated just for having this book available for your dog-owning clients.

═══ 15 ═══
BREAKFAST-IN-BED SERVICE

It's luxurious to be served breakfast in bed in a high-priced hotel; even more luxurious, and very often romantic, is being served breakfast in bed in your own home.

There's already a breakfast-in-bed service in New York City. The couple who run it come to your home or apartment at the appointed time (mostly weekends, though) and serve you a gourmet meal with wine, champagne or bloody Marys. Your bedroom becomes your own private dining salon.

A San Francisco man offers a service which appeals to former New Yorkers. On Sunday mornings, he delivers bagels and lox with all the trimmings: whitefish, onion, kosher dill, tomato and Greek olives. And a copy of the Sunday *New York Times*. Business is said to be brisk.

16
START A
TRADE SHOW OR FAIR

Trade shows and fairs have often been spinoffs of newsletters and magazines. On the other hand, newsletters and magazines have just as often been spinoffs of trade shows. All seem to start as spinoffs of someone's interest and imagination. And many make money.

Take the National Fashion and Boutique Show. Twice a year, manufacturers, distributors and mail-order houses cram their wares—which range from youth fashions (like dolled-up jeans and Hare Krishna blouses) to hash pipes and rolling papers—into the New York Coliseum. The same people also run shows in Chicago and Los Angeles. The "show'" is for the trade only—retailers come to buy—and many manufacturers and distributors attend the show to make deals.

Naturally, the Boutique Show didn't start that big. A few years ago it used only a few floors of the McAlpin Hotel. And there were far fewer visitors than the tens of thousands who now attend, studying the merchandise and ordering the latest for their shops and stores. The booths cost plenty to rent—so those who can't afford to rent an entire booth are carefully matched up by the show organizers with others who are in similar situations, so that even shoestring operations can afford to show their wares.

Rent money for the booths is required several months in advance, firming up the space requirements and giving the promoters plenty of working capital to pay rent and to do publicity. Press releases are sent to trade publications. Local advertising is placed. And invitations to attend are sent to shop and store owners across the country.

During the show, all visitors (and displayers) are required to register—all get badges (press, displayer, retailer, etc.). The registration gives the show an accurate count of how many people attended the show (to use in advertising for the next one); puts a copy of the show book into the hands of every visitor; and ensures that every visitor has seen the show's own booth —which is selling subscriptions to a *Boutique Magazine* published monthly by the show's organizers. Guards patrolling the show protect displayers and require every visitor to be registered. Registrations also build mailing lists for future shows.

The show book is free to all visitors—it lists each displayer and where to find the booth. It's also full of ads from displayers who desire multiple impact—the ad revenues pay for the book, which is a half-inch thick.

Shows, fairs and expositions have been set up all over the country to display just about everything. The key to success for every one of them has been great publicity—even notoriety. Shows are set up to display antiques even in the smallest towns; antique dealers and collectors from four states paid good money for the chance to hawk their wares to people around Riverton, Wyoming (population: 10,000), for example. The show's organizers charged admission, too.

Shows and fairs have focused on books, comic books, garden plants and equipment, comic art, soaps and bath supplies, autos, crafts, jazz, cooking, Beatlemania, boats, banjo picking, junior achievement projects, newsletters, newspapers and all kinds of industrial equipment. There are shows and conventions in almost every field—from military hardware to eyeglasses.

You may wish to start one involving your hobby. Equipment manufacturers, retail outlets, distributors, magazines and newsletters in the field, collectors, and craftspeople are all potential displayers. Carefully select your location for the show. Possibilities include hotels, coliseums, fairgrounds, colleges, barns, shopping center malls, and your own home and back yard (a comic-book show started in the organizer's Brooklyn home).

Consider the time of year that's best for your show. If you do a farm or construction industry show, for example, summer may be the worst time, since farming and construction are generally busiest in the summer.

Promote the show more than anything you've ever promoted in your life. Send press releases—every month, week or day—to every form of media available. Suggest feature ideas. If there's a farm angle on your comic-book show, send a specialized release to the farm magazines around.

Consider bringing in celebrities in the field—and charge a good admission price to the show. Promote your celebrities.

And be sure there are people who would want to come to such a show—a lot of such people locally. If there aren't, you're doomed. If there are, you've struck a gold mine—and one that will produce more and more every year you're in business.

OTHER IDEAS:

Organize block parties for retailers. They pay for your time and skill.

Candidates and issue-oriented organizations often pay organizers to plan parties, rallies and bashes.

Organizers are also contracted to coordinate openings and open houses for stores and other commercial establishments.

TO FIND OUT MORE:

The Exposition and Conference Council (c/o ANA, 155 E. 44 St., New York, NY 10017) has published three "White Papers" which may be valuable to the prospective exposition manager. They are on the subjects of Trade Show Security,

Trade Show Rules and Regulations, and Show Attendance Registration and Reporting.

How to Design and Decorate an Eye-Catching Booth (by Ben B. Berkey, Creative Book Co., P.O. Box 214998, Sacramento, CA 95821), though directed at the exhibitor, also presents ideas for the exposition director and publicist.

= 17 =
WELFARE

Welfare has always been controversial. Unlike people on unemployment, which is insurance workers pay for against the threat of future joblessness, welfare recipients take money from the state, which obtains most of its income from middle-class taxpayers.

Actually, the rich take more money than the poor; for every dollar spent on the poor, the government spends about three dollars on the rich. Government support for the rich includes subsidies for private airports so the rich can fly more cheaply, an inland waterway/canal built so that yachts could be transported across the country easily, and tax loopholes which result in tax money being uncollected by the government. But welfare is a frowned-on subsidy; for that reason, even some of the most destitute refuse welfare. They've been made to feel that accepting a government subsidy is a dishonorable act which would bring shame to their families.

Most welfare funds are disbursed as AFDC (Aid to Families with Dependent Children), which supports the young children of single or handicapped parents. Another large segment supports handicapped people or individuals who are chronically ill. A small amount goes to able people who cannot find work.

The problem with being on welfare is that it is bare subsistence. One welfare mother said, "I got two hundred and fifty dollars a month to raise three kids. Try to keep your life together doing that. It's like being in prison. One day I realized that anyone who's on welfare needs it, even if they think they are running a scam. They think they can get their life together but they really can't do anything else."

On the other hand, I know people who are on welfare and are living happy, satisfying lives without the tension of the rat race. They live simply, buy many items secondhand, and have plenty of time to pursue their life interests.

18
UNEMPLOYMENT INSURANCE

Unemployment insurance is a completely different ballgame from welfare. Having money does not disqualify you from collecting unemployment—in fact, we advise you to have a savings account for emergencies.

The difference is that unemployment insurance is set up solely to help those who are fired or laid off—who become unemployed through no fault of their own. You are paid a portion of your previous salary to keep you going financially until you're able to find another job. State laws vary, but you may be able to collect from six months to as long as a year and a quarter. You are required to look for work, and sometimes to report the half-dozen or more places you must approach each week.

TO FIND OUT MORE:

Many cities have lawyers' collectives, paralegal collectives and (pro-worker) radical organizations which will help you get onto unemployment and stay there—not always an easy feat. Check with your town's switchboard, People's Yellow Pages, or underground or alternative newspaper to find unemployment counseling where you live.

There are several books out on unemployment, and they're generally updated as the laws change. Reading at least one of them can be extremely helpful. Two good ones are *The Unemployment Handbook* (by Peter Jan Honigsberg, J.D., Ballantine, 1976) and *Your Legal Guide to Unemployment Insurance* (by Peter Jan Honigsberg, Golden Rain Press, P.O. Box 2087, Berkeley, CA 94702, 1975).

19
COFFEEHOUSE OWNER

When I was a child I dreamed of being associated with one of the salons described in French novels and Henry James' short stories. These were private clubs or patrons' mansions where the great men of letters, theoreticians and strategists, people about town, and weirdos met. Of course, on the other side of town, *Der Grune Cakadoo* catered to an assortment of petty thieves, revolutionaries, fugitives, ne'er-do-wells, probable killers, grave-robbers and, surprisingly, a number of decadent aristocrats who realized that they were all part of the show. Everyone was in costume.

In San Francisco, the Cafe Flore serves wines, teas and a

selection of coffees. Its limited food menu consists of a number of salads and sandwiches, several crepes and a delicious rich onion soup. The restaurant is surrounded with potted bromeliads and orchids which are for sale. Patrons sit looking at the streets of San Francisco through big windows, having animated discussions about the meaning of life. Additional tables outside are utilized on warm days.

In Berkeley, referred to variously as "the wave of the future" and "the open ward," the Caffe Mediteranium three blocks from the University of California campus has served millions of espressos, cappucinos, and machiatos to revolutionaries and reactionaries who all agree that the cafe's outrageously priced pastries are the best in town and that the tiny slices of cheesecake are delicious. In the back, a concessionaire runs a cafeteria-style kitchen. The cafe, started in 1957, is a large room, austerely decorated with a mural design on one wall and a waiting line at the coffee counter.

One Berkeley man fulfilled a dream by buying a coffeehouse that hadn't been making money. He turned it into a popular place by offering entertainment (music or poetry in the back room for a cover charge). You could always sit in the front room for the price of a cup of coffee. There was an ambience about the place which said that all were welcome, as long as they didn't bother the other patrons. The coffeehouse was successful until a brutal murder occurred in a clothing store two doors down and people avoided that block. After building business for two years, the cafe failed.

If you can create a mellow atmosphere where folks can find a peaceful place to converse and hang out, you may want to own a coffeehouse. But they take a long time to get established and sometimes they don't make money.

OTHER IDEAS:

Communes and large groups often find running a coffeehouse especially profitable because of the in-house source of labor.

Run a 24-hour community house which serves breakfasts, lunches, and dinners, then turns into a coffeehouse from 9 P.M. until 1 A.M., when it begins the day as a late-night restaurant.

Sell different coffees—Colombian, French Roast or your special house blend—by the pound, ground on the spot for home brewing.

TO FIND OUT MORE:

Tea and Coffee Buyers' Guide, Ukers' International (biennial; Tea and Coffee Trade Journal Co., 79 Wall St., New York, NY 10005) lists supply sources for coffees, teas, and related products and services.

The Book of Coffee and Tea (by Joel, David, and Karl Schapira, St. Martin's Press, 1974) is an excellent guide to coffees and teas. Includes how to roast your own, blends, recipes, etc.

The Coffee Book: A Connoisseur's Guide to Gourmet Coffee (by John Svicarovich, Stephen Winter, and Jeff Ferguson, Prentice-Hall, 1976) is also good.

Coffee: A Guide to Buying, Brewing and Enjoying (by Kenneth Davids, 101 Productions, San Francisco, 1976) covers how to choose coffee, what to taste for, how to roast, grind and brew it, espresso, coffee drinks and coffeehouse styles. Creative use of the information found here should at least double your business.

20
STREET AND PARTY ENTERTAINER

Corporations are hiring magicians, party hosts/hostesses are hiring clowns, and the streets are filled with the sounds of music. There's always a demand for entertainment, and with a little practice and the right props, almost anyone can become an entertainer.

Music is probably the hardest to learn. If you're considering playing or singing for money, you'd best be good at it already. On the steps of Sproul Hall in Berkeley, on the streets of New York, at Fisherman's Wharf in San Francisco, street musicians play jazz, classics, country, rock and folk on guitars, violins, trumpets, bagpipes, mandolins and a dozen other instruments. Each has an open instrument case or hat in front of him or her to collect the money. A few even employ a partner (preferably with guilt-tripping eyes and a good sense of humor) to personally pass the hat. A musician in the right place can easily pull in $10, $15 or even $20 in just a few hours.

Now improvise a bit. That's what Grimes Poznikov does. He plays his trumpet from inside a box psychedelically painted and labeled The Automatic Human Jukebox Machine. He parks himself in the box on Fisherman's Wharf. A tourist comes along, reads the signs (one says "The quality of the music is directly proportional to the amount of money you put in"), drops in some change and pushes two buttons to select a tune.

With a whistle, a flap on the box's front pops up and Grimes' head and trumpet pop out to play a tune. He has become so famous for the act that "To Tell the Truth" flew him to New York to stump the panel, and he is listed in the _TWA Black Book_ (the airline's guide to city entertainment). He's also made more than $50 on a good day. Location is important: Grimes tried to take the Jukebox Machine onto New York City sidewalks and parks and was consistently threatened with immediate arrest.

You don't have to be a rock band to play for parties. One fellow from Long Island, who performs in blue tails, a blue top hat and long skintight white gloves, has played piano at many a hip party in New York. Slip him ten dollars and he'll also improvise a striptease on the spot.

A Greenwich Village madrigal group sings at parties all over town. The singers wear inexpensive felt costumes they've made themselves and have the look of Robin Hood's band.

Henry the Fiddler goes to fiddle and country music festivals all over the country. He says that people recognize him wherever he goes, and he even sends out a newsletter to his fans each Christmas.

Many famous show business celebrites got their start playing small clubs for tips. Peter, Paul and Mary, Bob Dylan, and Lenny Bruce all were discovered while working in clubs for the "hat." While you don't earn a lot of money this way, it does help pay the rent.

One artist in Boston is famous for his street drawings. The police helpfully bar traffic from a street while he turns the thing from curb to curb into one huge Indian chalk "painting." Spectators throw money his way while he works; the painting remains on the street for several days (usually until it rains).

If you aren't already an artist or musician, don't despair. There are other forms of entertainment you can quickly learn. For example, become a magician, juggler, clown, ventriloquist, balloontwister, mime artist, organ grinder or puppeteer. Each of these can be practiced in the street with a hat or a helper to collect money. Or you can hire yourself out to parties and shows. Advertise in the Yellow Pages and with classified ads.

Use some imagination. Magicians, for example, are regularly being hired by large corporations to perform at trade and industrial shows. They also find themselves performing at adult and children's parties, schools, county fairs, store openings, block parties, shopping malls, local variety shows and many other local affairs, for $25 to $50 per show. The beginning magician can buy a stock of tricks and illusions that almost work by themselves for $100 to $200.

OTHER IDEAS:

Entertainers are frequently hired to perform at or organize children's parties. Come in costume (yours or as a clown, Easter bunny, gorilla, teddy bear, etc.), bring goodies, and share laughter.

Entertainers are also used to provide diversions and titillate conversation at adult parties. For instance, one couple hired out as "bickering mates." They are sure conversation starters.

You can also organize talent shows, community sings and events, performing or MC'ing each.

Don't forget to sell postcards of yourself.

TO FIND OUT MORE:

The Art of Juggling (by Ken Benge, World Publications, Box 366, Mountain View, CA 94042 1977) starts with the basics and heads into tougher patterns like the neck catch, the arm bounce and partners. It covers balancing items on one's forehead. And it discusses performing, from routining and presentation to showmanship and bits. It outlines props. And it offers a great deal of encouragement. Benge performs on TV and at stage shows across the country.

The Society of American Magicians (PR Director William

P. Dunbaugh, 4110 W. 109 St., Oak Lawn, IL 60453) has over 110 local clubs around the globe where members can hone their skills and learn new tricks from their contemporaries. It publishes the monthly *M-U-M*, free to members, which covers new tricks and apparatus, how to do many tricks and techniques, and interchange between all the clubs. It also offers members its free publicity service.

Clown of America (717 Beverly Rd., Baltimore, MD 21222) publishes a monthly magazine *Calliope*, filled with ideas, gags, skits and idea exchanges between members, as well as book reviews and features on various professional members. The association also publishes an informative how-to book: *Introduction to Clowning* by Karl "Whitey" Hartisch.

Puppeteers of America, Inc. (Box 1061, Ojai, CA 93023) draws together professionals, amateurs, hobbyists, and "just plain puppet fans." It publishes the bimonthly *Puppetry Journal*, periodic worksheets, and an annual membership directory; it holds regional and national festivals and workshops, and offers free consulting; it also has affiliated local guilds.

The Society of American Magicans (Lock Drawer 789, Lynn, MA 01903) is a worldwide professional association of magicians. Members get the society's full-size magic magazine, as well as a free publicity service. It has nearly 100 local chapters.

Magic: *The Great Illusions Revealed and Explained* (by David H. Charney, Plume Books/NAL, 1975) does a good job of revealing the tricks behind the big stage illusions: floating people, disappearing people, and others.

21
THERAPIST/COUNSELOR

Assertiveness Training. Est. Seminar on Initiating Relationships. Relaxation Specialist. Biofeedback. Gestalt. Exploring Human Sexuality. The Lilly Tank. Massage. Breath Awareness. Self-Esteem. Coping with Rejection. Transactional Analysis. Meditation.

Some people call it "therapy," others "growth," "personal growth," or "counseling." However it is named, we Americans love to learn more about ourselves, our relationships and our interactions. We explore relaxation and meditation and seek higher emotional, spiritual and mental levels.

Jim Spillane of Oakland, California, teaches weeknight and weekend classes in assertiveness training and initiating relationships, charging $20 per student. He also holds "Saturday Growth Seminars and Dances," which combine a daytime program of a dozen different growth workshops with an evening of dance. To attract students, he sends out direct-mail circulars about his programs. The parties he holds for graduates and their friends also attract students, as well as serving social and public relations functions.

Three years ago, a Waterloo, Iowa, couple who had been interested in personal growth for several years helped a university church group set up Human Sexuality Weekends. It led them to study Gestalt, assertiveness training, and sexual openness. Now they lead groups in each of those growth areas. They also lecture on sexual awareness and open marriage, do consulting work on organizational humanness, and lead sensitivity re-treats. Their side interest has become a career.

22
EMPLOYMENT COUNSELOR

In the process of writing this book, we've listened to the employ-ment complaints of hundreds of friends and acquaintances. We've asked them to list their skills and interests, as well as their employment fantasies. And we've made suggestions we thought they would enjoy trying. Sometimes those suggestions were employers and other times they were freelance jobs or businesses waiting to be started.

There are many books and courses about counseling and some colleges offer degrees in the field. The book you're hold-ing in your hands is one way to start counseling people on jobs and employment. Use it to run a psychological job-counseling service. Help your clients find out what they really want from their efforts and discover what means of livelihood are com-patible.

Market people's skills and interests for them. Or market jobs for employers. Get paid by taking some form of commission, either from the employer or the job-seeker. Promise the job-seeker job possibilities until he or she is happily employed, all for one price. Be an agent for jobs for your carpenter friend.

Specialize: A New York City woman has set up a job service

solely for business executives. Others specialize in older persons or teenagers, lawyers or craftspeople.

OTHER IDEAS:

Run group sessions on job interviewing using role-playing techniques or videotape to increase the skills of your clients.

Run a resumé service, designing and typing them for a fee.

Run a job collective which supplies all kinds of household workers.

23
PANHANDLER

Panhandlers work when they want or need to, meet people, work outdoors, and need no investment capital.

Panhandling may or may not be easy, depending on who and where you are. But the profession is worldwide.

At best, panhandling can be a fast way to put some money together. But it is temporary work. The panhandler who is successful pays close attention to dress, demeanor, his lines and the police.

Guilt and pity are proven moneymakers. Minority panhandlers often guilt-trip whites. In North Dakota, Indian panhandlers ask white tourists for dollar bills. They sometimes get them.

Outside Chicago's Museum of Science and Technology, a man hands pedestrians an inexpensive pen with a note: "I'm deaf and dumb. A donation would be appreciated."

In New York's Port Authority Bus Terminal, an attractive

young woman hustles men with, "My purse has been stolen and I *must* get back home to Philly. Please help."

Panhandling is discouraged in most localities because politicians feel that beggars present a poor image of the community.

══24══
GAMBLER

All of life is a gamble. But some things have better odds than others.

Successful gamblers have an inner confidence and a calculating mind as well as the fortitude and capital to withstand sudden reverses. They also have an appreciation for money and what it will buy.

Many people make a living hustling pool games. Bobby Riggs (who in his most famous appearance lost at tennis to Billie Jean King) has made a fortune hustling just about everything.

"Schwartzy" earns a living playing lo-ball, a poker game, at a legal card club in Emeryville, California. He usually plays the two- or five-dollar chip tables. But sometimes he'll take a shot at the twenty. "It's a different game, though—a different kind of player. Twenty-dollar players don't take the same kinds of chances."

If you're a winner, go ahead: Gamble for a living.

TO FIND OUT MORE:

The Facts of Blackjack is just one of the titles available from GBC Press, 630 S. 11 St., P.O. Box 4115, Las Vegas [where else?], NV 89106. Others include *Play Winning Poker, How to Bet the Harness Races,* and others on winning gin rummy, stud poker, keno, baccarat, roulette, slots, cribbage and more. Book list available.

=========================25=========================
TOUR GUIDE

A lone figure stands along the road, facing traffic entering New York City from the Hudson Tunnel. In his outstretched hand are three picture guidebooks to the city, and across his chest is a sign identifying him as "Tour Guide." Fifteen minutes later, he's in a car with a family of four, guiding them through Chinatown, headed for Wall Street.

If you like the city you live in, like telling other people about it, and want to learn more, become a tour guide. Your town doesn't have to be New York City. Do business people come to town? They're prime customers to guide around, since they're on expense accounts and often want to relax from the day's business by hitting the poshest restaurants, nightclubs and cocktail lounges your burg can offer. They'll pay you well ($35 to $70 for a few hours) and pick up your tab, too. List yourself with the Chamber of Commerce and get to know business, hotel, and convention center employees (give these last people a commission on any business they put you onto).

Foreign tourists are especially good prospects, and more foreigners are visiting the United States each year. Most have plenty of money to spend. Bilingual guides are always in demand. Charge by the hour and number of people—and expect tips. If you can lead technical or study tours, your fee should be higher than that for general guiding. Offer your services in person at the airport or through one of the many tourist guidebooks to local restaurants and nightclubs that are distributed free at major hotels. Find out what tourists want to see and offer to take them to theaters, museums, discotheques and watering spots.

But don't forget American tourists. Most Americans travel and carry plenty of cash to spend seeing the local sites. Just set up a sign that says "Tour guide, see historic Podunk." Place your brochures in motel literature racks. And get motel owners and operators to feed you customers—for a commission. Guide tourists in their own cars, showing them the highlights of your town. Remember that a family of five is going to want a different tour than will a business person away from his or her spouse.

Suppose there are neither tourists nor business people coming through your town. No matter. Guide local people through town. Some enterprising individuals in New York put this classified ad in a number of papers: "Re-educate your eyes. Visit New York City museums. Experienced guides. Call . . ." As long as you've researched local history, culture or architecture better than most people in town, you're qualified to show it to them.

You may want to write a speech you can read or you may want to ad-lib it. You may want to use your customers' vehicles or you may want to chauffeur them in your own car. Some cities require that tour guides be licensed, so check with the Chamber of Commerce. You may also need a business license.

If you don't want to work for yourself, work for others. Contact the local offices of charter and tour bus lines. Tour guides are often in demand with such companies.

You can also travel free and be paid, too, by becoming a tour escort. Companies which run escorted tours often advertise in newspaper travel sections and in the Yellow Pages. Your chances are best if you have traveled, speak a second or third language, and already have your passport.

While you're tour-guiding, you can make extra money by

selling maps, guidebooks, tourist guides, your own newsletter, books about local history, knickknacks and curious, and local crafts. Much of the literature is available free. You can get the rest wholesale.

OTHER IDEAS:

Offer guide services to organizations, interest groups, the handicapped, or businesses.

Children's groups, schools and harried parents (either local or touring) will love your daily and weekend educational children's touring service, designed to delight and amaze.

=====26=====
HOUSEWIFE/HOUSEHUSBAND

The concept of a housewife or a househusband is that of a partnership. Within the institution of marriage, the concept is rewarded by tax benefits: If both marriage partners earn high and equal incomes, they would be better off as singles living together; but if one marriage partner earns a high income and the other earns little or nothing, they get a tax break.

Of course, earning little or nothing doesn't mean that that partner does little or nothing. On the contrary, forming a workspouse/housespouse relationship can be both worthwhile and rewarding for the couple. Children are taken care of at no extra expense. The garden can provide food and lower grocery costs. And if the workspouse and the housespouse perform their working duties during the same time period, and then share in preparing and cleaning up after their common meals, they'll find they have quite a bit of leisure time afforded them to do with as they wish.

Many people find housework boring. But, says one house-husband, "If you're creative, you'll be able to get satisfaction out of everything you do, even vacuuming."

The advent of househusbanding is new and has come about as women have found higher-paying jobs.

The Martha Movement is a nationwide organization which has sprouted up from Washington, D.C., to improve the status of full-time homemakers. Local chapters are starting and a monthly newsletter is being published. The group also provides a free long-distance phone number for crisis calls and for getting in touch with other members of the group.

With the tax break, lower food and child-care costs, and increased leisure time, some couples will continue to choose house-spousing as one form of alternative workstyle which fits their needs. But this workstyle is definitely not for everyone.

27
PHOTOGRAPHIC OR ARTISTS' MODEL

University and college art classes hire models—both men and women—by the hour. The model is generally required to maintain a pose for students to sketch, and probably models partially or totally nude. A male student at Iowa State University earned all his spending money modeling in a jockstrap.

Professional artists and photographers also need models, and you don't have to be body-beautiful to qualify.

Talk of modeling connotes New York and high fashion. But most models work in their own home towns. If they become top models there, they then consider moving up the ladder to larger cities.

OTHER IDEAS:

Model in fashion shows put on by stores and manufacturers. You'll need poise and self-confidence and you should know (or learn) how to sell. Also, model clothing at conventions and resorts.

TO FIND OUT MORE:

Models Mart Ltd. (17 E. 48 St., New York, NY 10017) has an entire list of modeling books from its own presses as well as selected books from other publishers. These include *Everything You Wanted to Know About Modeling*, which stresses that the successful model must have basic physical attributes (this applies particularly in high fashion markets), lists the markets available for models, tells ways to get started, and offers helpful hints. There's *Call Me Mister* on deportment for men. And *How to Become a Successful Model,* which offers pointers on modeling of all types. Catalog is free.

28
PORNOGRAPHIC FILM STAR

Many people, especially young women and gay men, earn a living as porno stars. They work in full-length feature films, shorter skin flicks sold through porn shops, and budget-produced "loops" shown in peep-show theaters. Some work in "live sex acts" theaters, where sexual positions are simulated in an erotic display.

The pay may be low, less than $50 a performance, but, of course, some of the better-known pornographic film stars command large sums for movie appearances.

Film companies are located primarily in Los Angeles, New York and San Francisco. They occasionally advertise for auditions in alternative, underground, and sex newspapers.

OTHER IDEAS:

Work in a topless bar. Be a freelance go-go dancer.
Be a photographer's model.
Start a pornographic film collective.

29
KEPT MAN/KEPT WOMAN

Persons are kept—given free rent or space and sometimes food and allowances—for their companionship and sexual, sensual, or emotional services.

Most kept people are physically attractive and young. Sugar mommies and daddies—rich old people—often keep companions. But working people also keep playmates.

Sometimes there's marriage involved; other times, not. Often the relationship amounts to the kept allowing the keepers to have sex with them in order to maintain or increase their wealth, surroundings, belongings or status.

Being kept can be easy to do, well paying and possibly pleasurable. But like all situations, it is not for everyone.

30
TUTOR/INSTRUCTOR

Everyone has skills—they're used in hobbies, work and play. So why not teach your skills to others and make a little money doing it?

Can you swim or ski, sing, play the guitar, piano or other instrument, sail, play bridge, speak a foreign language, type or take shorthand? Can you do accounting, dance, do karate or judo, speed-read, play tennis, cook, play golf, exercise, paint, sculpt, do math, know physics or other sciences, sew, write, cartoon, skate, backpack, do magic or leatherwork, or have you had experiences which others can benefit from? Then you've go a subject to teach.

Teaching takes patience and skill. If you enjoy what you do, though, you'd probably have fun teaching it to someone else.

Offer your services to local school counselors and teachers. Place cards on bulletin boards around town (in supermarkets, drug stores, college student centers, public schools, etc.). School officials may have a list of tutors which is given to parents of kids who are having trouble learning—get your name added to the list.

Advertise in the classifieds. List your services or school in the Yellow Pages. Advertise on the radio. Pass out handbills. Place display advertising in the sports or society pages of the local paper.

Advertise, using slogans like "Special Low Rates" or "Most Comprehensive Instruction in Town" or something similar. If you're going to teach skiing, advertise with signs in shops which rent skis and winter sporting equipment (after all, your students will have to rent equipment somewhere, and you can put in a good word for the shops which help you get students).

You may wish to charge a little less than the established schools and instructors to get started. Charge more for private lessons than for class lessons.

You could soak up valuable techniques and information by taking classes from the established schools. You can learn about their instruction methods and their business procedures.

Promote. Demonstrate your skills at fairs, at school assemblies, at student centers, at resorts, in shopping center malls, during football and basketball game halftimes, or for talk or news programs on radio and TV. Write and send out press releases. If you've had any unusual experiences with your skill, emphasize them in one of the press releases; if your swimming skill saved someone from drowning, that's the basis for a news or feature story—even more so if the person you saved is now taking your swimming class.

You may wish to teach both beginning and advanced classes. Point this out in your promotion and advertising. Note that classes are a great way to make new friends. (Remedial tutoring and dancing lessons can be embarrassing for many people, so you might emphasize that private lessons are also available.)

Actually, you don't have to be skilled in any subject. Instead, you can go into partnership with or hire someone who is skilled in the subject. (You're offering the business and advertising acumen, which might make an interesting course itself.) If the instructing business grows, you could hire more teachers and increase your classes.

Think of the possible ways your students might profit from taking your class—and use it in your promotion and advertising. A person who knows a language, for example, has a much easier time when visiting a foreign country where that language is spoken. So advertise, "Visiting a Foreign Country? Your Trip Can Be Ten Times as Valuable if You Speak the Language." Put up signs in travel agencies, if possible. Give commissions for students they steer your way.

In some cities and towns there are "free schools" which act as clearinghouses between instructors and students. They publish monthly or semi-monthly catalogs, printed on newsprint. The catalogs are distributed free in stores, restaurants, and coffee-houses, and by mail. Course fees usually range from $15 to $40 per course, each comprising four 1½-hour sessions. Fees are often split 50-50 between school and instructor. Almost anyone with skills can register to teach or lead activities, and many instructors prefer this method of reaching potential students.

In the San Francisco Bay area there are at least six of these schools. Many of their courses overlap, but each has a distinct orientation. Heliotrope, the oldest, is a profit-making organization oriented to middle-class and family-centered individuals. It offers a range of classes in sports, business and professional skills, as well as "Christian Singles Weekends," various arts and crafts, specialty and ethnic cooking, party dancing and travel. It also offers self-improvement classes in assertiveness training, "fat liberation," transactional analysis, primal therapy, and Christian meditation.

Lavender U directs its services toward the large gay community. Its classes reflect the needs of the community it serves. Included are courses on gay liberation, homosexuality and society, and gay encounter, as well as dance, yoga, and self-improvement.

Lifeskool's classes include wine appreciation, 16mm sound production, screen printing, ballet, "dancercise" and basic auto maintenance. Self-improvement classes include meditation, T'ai Chi, astrology, trance and psychic development, Gestalt for women, biofeedback workshop, massage and backpacking.

Open Education Exchange's courses have a heavy emphasis on growth and holistic health. Some of them are bio-energy workshop, divorce recovery, sensory awareness, "how to get unstuck," bad-back seminar, relaxation and self-healing, tantric, prana, and hatha yoga, loving both sexes, and altering your sexual reality.

Orpheus' catalog places an emphasis on dance, drama and fitness. Courses include ballet, boogie, belly dancing, creative jazz, modern and sacred dance, mime, play production, body awareness and movement, jogging, aikido, karate, hatha yoga and legal highs.

Breakaway offers courses to women on assertiveness, skills, relationships, and more.

OTHER IDEAS:

Lead seminars, rap sessions and discussion groups.

If you are already earning a living from a craft, skill or profession, take apprentices. They may pay you or work for a reduced salary.

Have commercial establishments sponsor your instructing. For instance, a kitchen supplies shop might sponsor cooking classes and demonstrations.

Specialize in unusual classes such as knitting for men, carpentry and auto mechanics for women, playing for adults, independent living for the handicapped.

TO FIND OUT MORE:

Between Teacher and Child (by Haim Ginott, Macmillan, 1972) expresses the same humanistic and loving philosophy Ginott offers to parents in his other books. It's aimed at public school teachers, yet catches in its grasp all educators everywhere.

The Art of Teaching (by Gilbert Highet, Vintage Books, 1950): If this one's still in your library, read it. Though the methods are over two decades old, the insights into the roles of teacher and student still sparkle.

31

SPONSOR RETREATS AND WORKSHOPS

The President retreats with his senior advisors to Camp David. Business executives hold retreats. Social workers hold workshops. Churches hold retreats. Photography clubs, music schools, yoga and meditation groups, and nature watchers frequently sponsor workshops or retreats.

Individuals can also sponsor retreats or workshops. You can

also set up the retreats that religious, vocational and avocational groups hold.

You don't have to own land, but can rent both land and retreat space in the country. Church and civic groups sometimes have space to rent. You may want to arrange for a cook or for communal cooking. How rustic will your group go? Will they need blackboards and other materials from you? Should you provide recreational opportunities?

Answering those questions for each of the groups you schedule can earn you a living.

OTHER IDEAS:

Set up a "country place" for others to rent for retreats.

PART II
NATURE/
ECOLOGY

32

DOG WALKING
AND PET BOARDING

Jane Partridge and Julia Simmons walk dogs for a living. They take care of pets for people who don't have time to do it themselves. Others use the service when they go on vacation or leave for the weekend.

Jane and Julia started the business soon after they were laid off as receptionists during the 1969 Brokerage Firm Panic. "I didn't like working there anyway. I always felt like a piece of meat."

"We were roommates and we decided to go into business together. We knew we wouldn't work in an office again. Since we lived in a well-to-do neighborhood, our neighbors had the money to spend—and the problem. We put up signs on lampposts and in Laundromats and some stores. It was slow the first few months, but picked up as it got cold. I can walk six small dogs or three or four large ones.

"We will not take dogs that misbehave, are hostile or fight. We charge extra for bitches in heat. I used to charge one dollar for small dogs and one-fifty for large ones for an hour's brisk walk in the park; now we charge one-fifty and two twenty-five.

"Jane and I take turns. Each of us works three or four days a week. We both take vacations a lot. And, of course, being outdoors walking in the park is not the worst way to earn a living."

When their clients are away, J & J Service will also feed your pets, empty kitty litter trays, water your plants, and take care of mail and newspapers, charging about $9 per hour for the service. Their minimum charge is $1 to feed a pet they also walk.

"We have rescued several women from the office syndrome. We are so popular that we hired them to help service our clients' pets."

Many owners prefer to board their pets when they are away. Pet boarding can be a full-time business or a part-time supplement. I know a couple who are always caring for two or three pet guests. They charge $3 a day plus food, and work strictly by word of mouth. Other people have small licensed establishments with dog runs and troughs.

OTHER IDEAS:

Service fish tanks in commercial offices.

Run a pet-grooming service.

Offer pet-training services. You may wish to specialize in housebreaking pets or solving pet problems (compulsive barking and other neuroses).

Sell pet accessories like collars and warmers, rawhide sticks, toys, and more, as well as pet food, to your clients, or run a pet boutique.

TO FIND OUT MORE:

Care and Training of Your Puppy (by E. Fitch Daglish, Arco, 1976) includes sections on training, exercise and leash training, feeding, grooming, washing, trimming and illnesses.

Good Dog, Bad Dog (by Mordecai Siegal and Matthew Margolis, Holt, Rinehart and Winston, 1973) thoroughly covers dog obedience training and other problems, as well as individual training problems of 66 dog breeds.

33
GARDENER

If you'd like to be an artist who paints with plants on the canvas of other folks' lawns and grounds, then open your own gardening service.

You can be involved solely on the level of maintaining plants, flowers, lawns and grounds as they are. Or you can be involved with creating brand-new environments, landscapes, and exterior designs.

Either way, your tools will probably be fairly simple. Two Connecticut men set up their own gardening service to pay their way through architecture school. They purchased a pickup to haul plants and earth, hoes, shovels, and other tools. They custom-designed grounds according to their clients' desires and needs.

OTHER IDEAS:

Specialize in one type of garden. For instance, design and maintain Japanese gardens, ornamentals, food gardens, lawns or formal gardens.

34
LIVE BAIT SALES

Most people who fish, fish to relax, and they would rather spend more time at the trout stream and less time hunting bait. If you can provide them with big, juicy worms and nightcrawlers, crickets, grasshoppers, minnows, and other live bait at inexpensive prices, they'll pay you and thank you for it.

A Riverton, Wyoming, boy makes from $50 to more than $100 every week during the spring, summer and fall seasons selling nightcrawlers. Even then, the sign posted in front of his house often reads "sold out." He underprices his competition and hunts his bait on suburban lawns with a flashlight every night, turning up hundreds and thousands of "wigglies."

You can get into the business on a bigger level, too. A wholesale worm ranch near Casper, Wyoming, often has over 11 million worms on hand, worth perhaps $50,000 wholesale, for shipment to its retail outlets.

Minnows can also be easily caught and sold. And crayfish, maggots, mealworms and crickets can be easily raised and sold.

OTHER IDEAS:

Raise live food for pets. Fish eat tubifex or water worms, daphnia or water fleas, brine shrimp, goldfish and mealworms. Reptiles eat chicks, hamsters, mice and guinea pigs.

35
FOOD/HERB COLLECTOR

Fruits, herbs and spices are free for the taking in the wild, can be gleaned from orchards and fields, and are given away by some markets and fruit stands. How ironic that these free-for-the-taking foods rot unused while the supermarket down the block sells them at outrageous prices. And if the supermarket can sell them for profit, so can you.

Johnny Wahaikii is a retired cowboy living near the town of Hana, Maui, Hawaii. When he needs spending money, he gathers mangos, passionfruit, bananas and coconuts which grow wild around his house and sells them to tourists. "These no Chiquita bananas; they ripened on the tree. These passionfruit—you eat one a day, never have cold. Oh, I go get these this morning," he said, pointing to a half bushel of assorted fruit. "In hour they be gone and I go home."

Of course, Johnny lives on a tropical isle known for its prolific vegetation. But there are crops for the picking or gathering everywhere. Another enterprising fellow named John, in Medford, Oregon, gathers mushrooms during the long rainy season. He dries them and sells them to gourmet stores in San Francisco.

The Heath family (all seven of them) go berry-picking all summer long. They sell the fruits of their labors to grateful neighbors.

Tons of ginseng root are gathered every year in the Appalachian Mountains. They are sold to dealers for export to Korea. (Processing ginseng in the U.S. could be a profitable industry.)

Across America, streets and yards are littered with edibles each autumn. Walnuts, hickory nuts, filberts, almonds, apples, pears, peaches and apricots are often swept away by street cleaners as a nuisance.

Edible Wild Plants, Feasting Free on Wild Edibles, Field Guide to Edible Wild Plants, Foraging for Wild Edible Mushrooms and Mushroom Hunter's Field Guide are just a few of the dozens of books available on gathering herbs and edibles from the wilds. Some of these plants are considered gourmet items, but are rarely available commercially. Gourmet stores and restaurants will gladly buy these delicacies.

Some enterprising apple and pear growers have discovered that they can make more money letting consumers pick their own fruit than by selling to wholesalers. They charge by the hour or bushel and everyone comes out ahead, since the consumers buy direct. Other farmers let people glean their fields and orchards after the commercial harvest. Excess fruit can be canned, dried or frozen.

The Phoenix, Oregon, Farmers Market gives away bruised fruit all summer long. People use the fruit as animal feed and for pies and fruit salads. But one individual slices out the damaged portions and dries the good parts in his solar dehydrator. He trades the fresh, organically dried fruit for other food at the local community food store.

He also dehydrates tomatoes and uses the dried pieces for tomato sauce; slices zucchini squash with a potato peeler and uses the dried pieces as organic chips; and evaporates watermelon juice for use as natural sugar.

The common snail found in northern California is actually the French gourmet snail (escargot). It was imported by the owner of a French restaurant and escaped, adapting easily to its new home and becoming a garden pest. Some people gather them, feed them a diet of lettuce and cornmeal for a week to clean out their systems, and cook them in a tangy sauce.

While snails are not to everyone's taste, there are sources of food and income all around you.

TO FIND OUT MORE:

Profitable Herb Growing at Home (by Betty E. M. Jacobs, Garden Way Publications, Charlotte, VT 05445, 1976) is a complete guide to growing and marketing herbs and herb products.

Wild Foods Cookbook and Field Guide (by Billy Joe Tatum, Workman Publishing, 1976) is split: part one shows you 70 wild plants with pictures, descriptions, and commentary on when and what to harvest; part two describes how to fix your gleanings, which should help sales.

Wildcrafting: Harvesting the Wilds for a Living (by Jack McQuarrie, Capra Press, 631 State St., Santa Barbara, CA 93101, 1975) covers the author's recommendations on gathering brush and forest shrubbery, forest decoratives, fruit, wild edibles, seed cones, bark, herbs, worms, pollen and moss. He's done it. His is also a beautiful book.

36
IMPORT/GROW/
DEAL MARIJUANA

Marijuana is illegal. Yet its cultivation, importation and sales are said to be a 10-billion-dollar industry, so large that the associated paraphernalia business (pipes and papers, for the most part) is itself a 200-million-dollar business. There are probably between one and two million people in the United States earning at least part of their incomes from growing, importing and dealing marijuana.

Dealing is basically a system of distribution—buying a large quantity, dividing it into smaller lots, and reselling it.

Dealing is a risky business; thousands are in jail in the United States and abroad for possessing and dealing pot. Laws and enforcement vary from state to state and community to community.

Dealing is also very tricky; survival depends on knowing the many different types of marijuana, each with its own potency and effects, ranging in price from $30 a pound to over $200 an ounce.

Dealing as a way to earn a living can be interesting, boring, fast, slow, comfortable or neurotic. It depends on the individual. Dealers spend most of their time making contacts to buy and sell, and testing quality. They meet all sorts of people whom they probably would never come into contact with had they decided to become retail clerks.

On even the lowest level, there is room for terrific profit. A pound of high-quality Mexican may cost $150. Ounces sell for $15 each. One ounce is usually used for testing, leaving 15 ounces to sell, for a total of $225. People who start out as small retailers often work their way up the chain and become large wholesalers. Marijuana is one product that literally sells itself; users are always interested.

Dealers sometimes specialize in specific operations and work together to do their deals. For instance, a smuggler might work with a pilot or runner, as well as a trucker and a wholesale distributor, on a particular operation. Large dealers sometimes hire salespeople to work for them on a commission basis.

Some people grow large quantities of marijuana and sell their crops. One San Franciscan uses a spare room to grow 32 plants. He has a new crop maturing every two months and harvests enough smoke from each crop to sell about $200 worth. Other people grow outdoors. You can grow 10 to 20 pounds (at $100 a pound, that comes to one or two thousand dollars) in a large garden. Beware of thieves and police.

OTHER IDEAS:

Dealing cocaine involves both higher profits and much higher risks.

Several midwestern hash oil factories use local ditch grass, extracting the resins and converting them to high-potency oil.

Some dealers make marijuana brownies, candy or cakes for sale at fair and craft shows. These products have a much higher profit margin than your usual chocolate chip cookie.

Many people gather or grow psilocybin mushrooms. They are relatively easy to grow, and kits are advertised in national magazines. The dried mushrooms sell for as much as $150 an ounce. They can be gathered in many areas of the country from Florida to Washington State.

A major source for mescaline is the people who gather or import peyote buttons or grow San Pedro cactus.

TO FIND OUT MORE:

The Indoor-Outdoor Highest Quality Marijuana Growers Guide (by Mel Frank and Ed Rosenthal, And/Or Press, Berkeley, CA, 1975) is the best early book on marijuana cultivation.

Marijuana Growers Guide (by Mel Frank and Ed Rosenthal, And/Or Press, Berkeley, CA, 1977) is the most important book ever published on marijuana cultivation. A veritable bible, it contains the most up-to-date information and easy-to-follow directions ever assembled to assure the success of a marijuana crop.

Weed: The Adventures of a Dope Smuggler (by Jerry Kamstra, Bantam, 1975) is a great autobiography.

Dealing; or The Berkeley-to-Boston Forty-Brick Lost-Bag Blues (by Michael Douglas, Alfred A. Knopf, 1971) was both a novel and a movie; it does a marvelous job describing a medium-sized, low-key dealing operation.

For current information on narcotics agents and their techniques, as well as on drugs and drug prices, read *High Times* (Box 386, Cooper Station, New York, NY 10003) magazine. It's on most newsstands.

37
PROSPECTOR/GOLD PANNER

In some areas of the United States, precious rocks and minerals such as gold and jade can still be found lying on top of the ground or in streams and stream beds.

Prospecting and panning for gold are usually hard jobs which pay about the same as labor—$3 to $5 per hour. But the hours are those you choose, and you get to spend them outdoors where skies are blue, the air is (almost) pure, and the scenery is often straight from a picture postcard.

One prospector in west central Wyoming, for example, makes about $4 for each hour he puts in panning for gold in mountain streams. He likes small towns and the aloneness of the mountains. He may catch trout from the same stream he pans for gold. His expenses are low, since he lives out of a tent, but he finds that Wyoming mountain seasons allow him to pan only three months a year.

OTHER IDEAS:

Look for semiprecious stones and rocks for collectors and lapidaries.

Prospect for large concentrations of metals or minerals.

TO FIND OUT MORE:

The Western Gem Hunters Atlas: Rock Locations from California to the Dakotas and British Columbia to Texas (by Cy Johnson & Son, Box 288, 435 N. Roop St., Susanville, CA 96130; revised periodically): 80 pages of maps to lead you to finds of gemstone.

Uranium: Where It Is and How to Find It (by Paul Dean Proctor, Edmond P. Hyatt, and Kenneth C. Bullock, Eagle Rock Publishers, Salt Lake City, 1954) is old and small, but well done. There are still a few uranium finds being made these days. This book could be very helpful.

Let's Go Prospecting! (by Edward Arthur, P.O. Box 395, Joshua Tree, CA, 1970) is slightly California-oriented but will give you a good overview of prospecting as avocation or vocation. Covers black-light prospecting, uranium, gold, gems and industrial minerals and metallic ores.

══ 38 ══
JUICE MAKER

Fresh juice has a distinctive taste that no canned or frozen product can duplicate. But it's hard to find in groceries and supermarkets.

In Ashland, Oregon, a fellow started the Pyramid Juice Co., which sells freshly squeezed carrot juice. He juices the carrots early each morning and bottles the juice in quart and gallon containers. It is delivered to stores the same morning. He also supplies several restaurants and a fruit stand.

The juice sells for $1.50 a quart, including a 20¢ deposit on the bottle. He pays the stores 30¢ of the price for each quart that they sell, and takes back any unsold juice. Of course, the juice is kept refrigerated, since no preservatives or pasteurization are used.

When he first started the business, he bought carrots wholesale. Now he buys many of his carrots direct from farmers.

While most groceries do not sell fresh juice, some of them would like to. Fresh carrot, orange, and apple juice are probably the most popular. You could also make blends, or use tropical juices such as papaya, pineapple, mango or tangerine. Health-food stores, restaurants and fruit stands are all good retail outlets for your product.

To start you will need an electric vegetable juicer or orange juicer, a van or station wagon to truck in fruit and deliver juice, and appropriate licenses. Possibly you could work out an arrangement with a local restaurant to use their facilities early in the morning when the place is closed.

A relatively small business can be very profitable. Selling 100 quarts a day, for example, means a gross of $100 a day. At least a third of that will be profit.

Some enterprising individuals have set up juice stands at busy locations for on-the-spot consumption. In New York City there's a juice stand at 14th Street and Second Avenue. It's just a little hole in the wall, but it sells lots of juice. Mobile juice stands do well at fairs, rock concerts, and other events.

Juice-making is one of the few get-rich-quick ideas in this book. A motivated individual can build a juice company into a million-dollar business in a couple of years. But it requires commitment, a keen business sense, and sales ability.

If you can get your product into supermarkets, you may be able to sell thousands of quarts a day.

OTHER IDEAS:

Once you have opened up a market for juice, you can sell other products to your customers. Obvious foodstuffs include homemade bread and baked goods, candies, spaghetti and chili sauces, and salad dressings.

Sell your products to milk delivery route owners, or set up your own retail delivery service.

39
FISHERPERSON

For decades, America's daydreams featured small boys playing hooky from school and older boys (grown men) calling in sick, and then going fishing. To go fishing whenever one chose was thought of as the easiest-going, laziest lifestyle possible.

But fishing may be a growth industry in the next few years. The per capita consumption of fish is up and foreign trawlers face a 200-mile restricted fishing zone, increasing the opportunities for U.S. citizens.

Fishing was one of the earliest means of food-gathering, and has been an occupation ever since. My great-grandfather in Iowa helped his family through the Depression by fishing the Cedar River, selling part of his daily catch and bringing the rest home for dinner.

Check your local laws: fishing for sport is allowed in every state, but fishing for profit is often regulated or restricted. You'll undoubtedly need at least one license to fish at all.

OTHER IDEAS:

Go crabbing, clamming, etc.

Build a pond or tank and grow fish. Not only can you sell the fish, but the fishpond water, within a garden, can form a complete ecosystem.

Be a fisher-guide to "the best" fishing spots.

Run a fishing-boat service for sports-fisherpeople.

Clean fish for a living. Many sports-fisherpeople are happy to pay someone to clean their catch. In addition to paying you, they may also let you keep "trash fish," which often have some resale value.

40
NATURE COLLECTOR

Rocks, flowers, seashells, fossils, cattails, driftwood, bark, tree limbs, pine cones, cast-off wood, weathered wood, pine needles . . . Nature is all around you, free for the taking. Even better, it will stay free for the taking for many, many years to come. And it can make you a living, either as is or transformed into something else.

Take the rock, for example. Beautiful rocks can be sold as is. Or they can be cut, tumbled or polished. Little rocks can be made into jewelry—earrings, tieclasps, pendants, key chains, cufflinks—the list is endless. Paint flowers or frogs on small flat rocks (decorator rocks). Paint jokes on flat rocks with "Turn Me Over" painted on top and the punch line on the reverse side. Or how about a whole line of greeting-card rocks? ("Would you believe greeting rocks?")

You could paint owl faces on small rocks, and glue them on small limbs (perhaps staining the wood), so that the owls (or frogs or whatever) are staring at each other. Or decoupage pictures of cowboys, bakers or candlestick makers onto rocks (by gluing the picture onto the rock with white glue, then covering rock and picture with multiple layers of thinned white glue and a final layer of artist's fix).

The entrepreneur who packaged the "Pet Rock" ("requires no pet food, rolls over down hills, but can't shake hands") is a millionaire today.

Make cornhusk dolls. Poke dried flowers into hay cubes. A Wyoming artist nails a cowboy's picture, an empty Copenhagen tobacco can, a jeans back pocket, a horseshoe, etc., in any arty combination on a foot of weathered wood, with a leather strap on top for hanging. Make driftwood into lamps— or sell as is. Dip pine cones into chemicals to burn in rainbow hues when thrown into fireplaces. Paint pine cones. Sprinkle them with glitter. Or just sell the pine cones as they are.

Lee Heflin, in San Francisco, makes "God's Eye" mandalas measuring four feet across using feathers glued onto plywood. He can make one in two or three days and charges $750 to $1000 each.

Glass the tops of old sewing-machine drawers and fill them with beans, grains, seeds, tiny toy tractors: sell them as wall hangings. Iowa artists use old sewing-machine or printer's-type drawers for picture frames to display cornhusk dolls and dried flower arrangements. Turn a brandy snifter, dirt, flowers, rocks, and whatever into a terrarium.

Create Christmas displays, wreaths, flower arrangements, centerpieces with pine branches. Decoupage pictures, paintings, wedding announcements onto weathered wood, scrap lumber, tree bark. Make permanent flower arrangements of dried leaves and dried flowers glued on large flat rocks.

Most of all, though, use your imagination and your creativity. You'll do fine.

41
HORSE SHOER

The number of domestic horses in the U.S. is increasing, and with it the need for horse shoers, farriers or smiths.

A small-town farrier probably doesn't work out of a livery stable or out of a blacksmith's shed. Instead, a northeast Iowa horse shoer carries all his tools in the back of his pickup, which he uses to meet his appointments.

Horse shoers are in demand everywhere. In New York City, for example, there is a shortage of "shoers" to service horses in rental stables. The New York City Police Department had to search nationwide to replace a retiring smith.

To learn the trade, apprentice to a farrier.

OTHER IDEAS:

As a farrier, you come into constant contact with horse owners. Provide other goods or services which horse owners buy.

Become a horse-trading and breeding information specialist.

Become a horse buyer and travel the country choosing the "right" horses for your clients to buy; you arrange the terms for their approval.

TO FIND OUT MORE:

How to Shoe a Horse (by Marion C. Manwill, Arco, 1976) is the ideal guide to the subject. It not only covers horse-shoeing thoroughly but also foot physiology, foot problems, and corrective shoeing.

⟪42⟫
PLANT NURSERY

You can grow plants almost anywhere. But then, if you like plants, you already know that. If that's the case, consider starting a plant nursery: selling or renting plants can make you money.

With a little ingenuity, a garden, lot, spare room, basement, hallway, closet, enclosed porch, window or skylight can be turned into a nursery. If you have space, you can construct or buy an inexpensive greenhouse. The space needs to be well ventilated, within easy access of water, and well lighted. If the area you select is poorly lighted, use fluorescent lights. The amount of light needed varies tremendously with the variety of plant. You could also use dimly lit space to grow plants which require less light. Sprouts and mushrooms, for example, need little light.

Consider concentrating on one type of plant. If you have a greenhouse you might raise fast-growing plants such as coleus, begonia, caladiums, sweet potatoes or wandering jews. In a matter of a few months, clippings or bulbs will grow large enough to sell as decorator plants for $5 to $15.

Another possibility is growing small rooted cuttings. Large plants constantly produce clippings which can be turned into 50¢ items.

Some growers specialize in one species of plant—orchids, African violets, bromeliads, geraniums or ferns; others grow seedlings for outdoor replanting. Marigolds, tomatoes (especially hybrids, which are in great demand), peppers, squash and herbs are all sold by nurseries. Since nurseries get most of their stock from large growers, you can grow novelty varieties which are not generally available. Hybrid tomatoes, unique squashes and unusual spices all have good marketability and draw premium prices.

There's a good and growing market for living and dried esoteric herbs: gotu kola, ginseng, camomile and jasmine are all in demand. These herbs can be grown outdoors or indoors in many parts of the country. Staghorn ferns will grow in dim light against spare walls. There's a fortune being made in bonsai trees. And mushrooms can be grown in a controlled environment (basements may make good mushroom beds).

Some people set up their growing units so that they sell plants seasonally; for instance, shamrocks for St. Patrick's Day, Easter lilies for Easter, lily-of-the-valley in the spring, caladiums in the fall, poinsettias for Christmas, and flowering bulbs in winter are profitable seasonal offerings. Other people specialize in plants which will get you high: legal-to-grow highs like jimson weed, tree datura, coffee, cocoa, wild lettuce and lobelia (all legal in most states), or illegal plants such as psilocybin mushrooms, coca, peyote and marijuana. One grower made a fortune selling Thai marijuana seedlings for transplanting.

As with any business, you must know your market, your competition, and the economics of the situation.

You will gross more by selling your plants directly to customers, since nurseries and stores buy at discounts ranging between two-thirds and one-half of retail. You can sell plants to friends and neighbors, at craft fairs, through community food stores, at garden/garage sales, at flea markets, through local papers and, best of all, by word of mouth.

You can also rent out plants. There are plant-rental services in cities all over the country. They usually rent and service large plants for offices, although they will also supply plants for parties and other special occasions. You can buy these plants from a wholesale house and rent them to commercial establishments in your area.

Or you can board plants. There is a woman in Youngstown, Ohio, who fills her greenhouse with other people's plants each summer. She started boarding plants eight years ago when several of her neighbors went on extended vacations. Over the years, she has developed quite a trade. She also acts as a houseplant doctor.

There are lots of ways to do it: If you have a green thumb, you may as well have a green pocketbook.

TO FIND OUT MORE:

Under Glass (P.O. Box 114, Irvington, NY 10533) is small, but dedicated to better greenhouse gardening. Its 24 pages each month suggest the flowers which should be planted for the season, detail several flowers and how best to grow them, offer hints, tips and reviews, and through classifieds list mail-order sources for plants and products.

The $29.95 Greenhouse (by Luciano and Chuck Koehler, Hidden House, Palo Alto, CA, 1977) describes a 5′x10′x6′ greenhouse which can be built in a day to extend your growing season by several months.

There are innumerable books on growing plants and running nurseries. The U.S. Department of Agriculture has available a catalog of books and booklets in all of these areas. State and county extension agents may also be able to help you.

43
PET BREEDING

Janet, like a growing number of Americans (particularly single Americans), owns and loves a dog. She walks Coby three times a day and, she admits, in many ways Coby runs her life.

But Coby is more than just a pet; she is a registered Old English Sheep Dog. Janet has bred her twice with a suitable registered Old English Sheep Dog stud. Coby had four pups the first time, and eight the second. The pick of both litters went to the owner of the stud, as a fee. After that was done, the first litter sold for $725, and the second for $1250.

OTHER IDEAS:

Breed fish and sell them to other collectors or stores.

Breed hamsters, mice, rats or guinea pigs for sale as pets or to laboratories.

Breed registered cats; they appeal to sophisticated cat fanciers.

44
FARMER

Farming requires land ownership. Either have enough money to buy the land outright, or plan to work a well-paying job or business until the land is paid for. One communal group formed a construction company in Ames, Iowa, and built a number of buildings (mostly restaurants and bars) there to pay for its 80 acres of Missouri farmland.

Once you own the land, your lifestyle is your own. Most subsistence farmers recommend raising a little of everything for your own use, as well as one or two cash crops, from cucumbers or grapes to sweet corn, honey (beekeeping), or timber. Or your cash crop could be entirely different—crafts, for example, or artwork. One Tennessee man writes articles as his cash crop.

Cannabis (marijuana) is a cash crop that's risky but rewarding. It's being grown on both subsistence and commercial levels in every section of the United States.

OTHER IDEAS:

Lease garden plots on your farm to city dwellers who come up on weekends to tend their crops. A California man leases his 4000 orange trees, usually one to a customer (a tree may yield 160 pounds of oranges). He'll even pick the fruit and ship it to out-of-area customers.

Farm earthworms. They pass waste and soil in tiny deposits called castings, valuable as fertilizer. They turn any dirt into fertile black earth.

Become a custom slaughterer. These men and women call on farm and ranch owners to shoot, gut, skin and clean a head of beef or pork for farm family use.

Be a freelance sheep shearer.

TO FIND OUT MORE:

The Mother Earth News (P.O. Box 70, Hendersonville, NC 28739) is the ideal sourcebook for subsistence farming. It will tell you about tools and plants and animals. Get a list of back issues and order the ones you need. Or check them out in the library.

The Manual of Practical Homesteading (by John Vivian, Rodale Press Book Division, Emmaus, PA, 1975) is jam-packed with information on raising vegetables, crops and animals.

First-Time Farmer's Guide (by Bill Kaysing, Straight Arrow, 1973) is an idea book as well as an introduction to land, water, soil, plants, tools, energy and resources.

Homesteaders Handbook (by Rich Israel and Reny Slay, P.O. Box 596, San Francisco, CA 94101, 1973) is another packed-with-useful-information handbook for getting back to the land.

MOONSHINER

Moonshining, though illegal (or perhaps because it's illegal), is one of the most successful businesses operating in the United States today. "Squeezins" are still being produced by clandestine one-person stills hidden away in the Smoky Mountains. And in cities, the feds have turned up stills in garages, warehouses, barges, houses, boathouses, and spots as unlikely as churches.

Moonshiners do well because taxes keep the cost of alcohol artificially high. There's demand for moonshine because it's cheap—often ranging from a fourth to half the price of legal whiskey—and because customers like its powerful taste.

It is estimated that one of every eight whiskey drinks served in the United States is moonshine. The moonshine poisonings which are occasionally reported are the result of poor quality control or improper equipment. By maintaining high standards, moonshiners assure their customers' repeat business.

OTHER IDEAS:

Some people brew their own quality beers or wines and sell them to friends and neighbors.

TO FIND OUT MORE:

An Essay on Brewing, Vintage and Distillation, Together with Selected Remedies for Hangover Melancholia; or, How to Make Booze (by John F. Adams, Doubleday, 1970) covers not only wine and beer, but also booze (distilled spirits) and honey mead.

Quality Brewing: A Guidebook for the Home Production of Fine Beers (by Byron Burch, Joby Books, 441 Lexington, El Cerrito, CA 94530, 1975) is a short but authoritative primer on brewing your own beers and ales, some recipes, and the principles involved.

Guide to Better Wine and Beer Making for Beginners (by S. M. Tritton, Dover, 1969) will tell you what to ferment, how to ferment it, brewing, recipes, blending, bottling and storing.

46
POLLUTION FINK

Over the past 200 years, America the Beautiful has become America the Industrial. There are still unspoiled areas, but across the land skies reek of gray and brown smoke, and streams and rivers and even the ocean are filled with garbage, chemicals and raw sewage. The land is covered with litter. And it's so noisy in some places that shouting is the only form of communication.

Much has been done to clean up the environment, but we have a long way to go. You can help in the cleanup and get paid for it, too—because polluters can be and are prosecuted—and fines imposed are often split with the finks.

Take air pollution. In New York City, Citizen's Complaint forms are available by calling the Department of Air Resources. The citizen filing one may be eligible for a bounty of 25 to 50 percent of any fine placed against the polluter.

Black smoke is totally prohibited in New York City, except for an initial blast of 15 to 30 seconds. And the Department of Air Resources trains "smokewatchers" in official smoke observation, the law, combustion, and identification of visible emissions. They compare the blackness of smoke emitted with a card printed with a series of grays from very light to black, and determine whether or not the emitter is in violation.

It's not the easiest thing to prove, but numbers of New Yorkers walking the streets with extra cash generously "donated" by polluters are living proof that it can be done.

Water pollution is easier to prove. First, backtrack the pollution to determine its origin. Some bounty hunters have tried rowing upstream in canoes to track down pollution sources. Others have used food-coloring dyes at the source to trace and prove pollution and its dispersion. Samples of bad water with records of when, where and how the samples were collected make good evidence. Take photographs and get written statements from all witnesses. Then present your evidence to your regional U.S. Attorney, tell him/her you're bringing a complaint, and ask for prosecution under the 1899 Refuse Act.

Many firms engage in illegal dumping of solid waste. These cases are often easy to prove.

Noise pollution is the hardest to prove. It's nearly impossible to collect bounties by turning in noise polluters—unless you're an aural engineer. It takes tremendous technology and a working knowledge of it to be able to collect the kind of evidence needed to bring a complaint against a noise polluter.

No matter what polluter you'd like to turn in, know the law —what's against the law, why it's against the law, and how to file a complaint correctly. Sometimes a disgruntled corporate employee will help you with your case by supplying you with inside information and internal memoranda. Since officials are often reluctant to prosecute pollution cases, your chances of convicting a company and cashing in on fines are much better if you know your rights from the start. You may even need your lawyer to force the government to prosecute.

It's possible to earn a living at polluter bounty hunting. Some of the awards to hunters have been in excess of $10,000 on a single case. Other cases have involved a fine for each day the law is violated. Corporations sometimes absorb these penalties as a cost of doing business.

As in all litigation, these cases are time-consuming, take much research, and require astute technical and legal skills, especially the first time around. Of course, with the knowledge and skill you gain on your first prosecution, the second time will be easier.

TO FIND OUT MORE:

Agencies to check with on permits to pollute, laws against pollution, and evidence required to prosecute include environmental action groups, the local Army Corps of Engineers, the U.S. Attorney's Office, the U.S. Environmental Protection Agency, local county and state Departments of Air Resources, and Environmental Conservation Control Boards. Environmental groups and public interest research groups can often help you obtain needed information.

How to Stop the Corporate Polluters and Make Money Doing It (by William H. Brown, from the *Mother Earth News* Bookshelf, P.O. Box 70, Hendersonville, NC 28739) tells you more about using the 1899 Refuse Act in fighting polluters and collecting your share of the fines against them.

47
EXTERMINATOR

In large cities, the pests you'll run up against the most are roaches. The answer is boric acid: sprinkle it along the baseboards of all walls, under the edges of carpets, runners and rugs, along the insides of cupboards and drawers, and across all roach runways. The roaches get the powder on their legs, lick it off, then disappear and die—for up to six months at a time. Yet, despite the fact that boric acid is one of the most effective roach deterrents around and despite the fact that it can be purchased in any drugstore, most people won't or don't use it. One natural-pesticide company is repackaging it (adding a trace of some mystery ingredient) and labeling it with a brand name that conjures up images of dead roaches; the product is selling quite well.

When you use a product in a household, be aware of and avoid harming pets and children.

Most pest control training is done by the individual pest control companies, both in classrooms and on the job. People who apply pesticides must be certified by their state, or work under direct supervision of someone who is certified.

TO FIND OUT MORE:

National Pest Control Association, Inc. (8150 Leesburg Pike, Suite 1100, Vienna, VA 22180) publishes dozens of books and materials on pest control, management, public relations, and safety. Prices run three times higher for non-members.

Write the pesticide companies for their information.

Household Insect Pests (by Norman E. Hickin, St. Martin's Press, 1974) spends a great number of pages on identification and only a few on control; it also ignores the boric acid cockroach treatment, advising instead that a pest-control company should be called in for cockroach infestations. Nevertheless, it offers some valuable information on controls.

48
PRODUCE GARDEN
IN MOVABLE CONTAINERS

Most city dwellers seem to think that growing flowers or vegetables requires expensive greenhouses. Yet all around them, everywhere, even in the smallest cities, are unused empty lots and apartment-house rooftops. Often the empty lots are lying idle for speculation, tax purposes or proposed construction, or are just abandoned.

You can use empty lots and rooftops to grow flowers or vegetables in movable containers. First get the owner's or manager's permission. Stress the fact that your containers can be removed from the site on short notice.

The land should have access to water, and enough light to maintain healthy vigorous plants. If you are permitted, you can erect a portable greenhouse. It will extend the growing season, increase rate of growth, and reduce the amount of water and watering needed.

Find your containers—it's no problem. Vegetable stands sometimes throw out bushel baskets and restaurants discard one- and five-gallon cans and buckets as well as occasional 25- and 55-gallon drums. Other containers to consider include wooden packing crates, waterproof boxes, and bathtubs. Remember that the garden should be movable. Some people place the containers on pallets so they can be moved with a forklift.

Next, choose a growing medium. Empty lots are usually

paved over or have poor soil. You can buy or dig topsoil, use construction sand and fertilizer, or make compost.

Substantial amounts of organic matter suitable for composting are available from restaurants, vegetable markets, food-processing plants, city leaf collections, and other sources. Plan what to plant. Your location and market should determine your products. Some plants that do well in containers include tomatoes, peppers, beans, peas, houseplants, radishes, some herbs, and many kinds of flowers. If the lot has poles or structures you may wish to suspend hanging plants from wires.

This garden can provide subsistence or better. Cultivated plants are highly prolific and yield tremendous quantities in small spaces. Plants and vegetables can be sold to retail customers, stores and restaurants.

OTHER IDEAS:

Lease empty lots for gardens. You can work them yourself or sublet plots to gardenless urbanites. Offer to pay a lot owner a commission on your produce sales instead of a monthly rent.

Government agencies have started funding community garden projects.

Use "garden space" to farm fish or other small livestock, such as rabbits or chickens. Aquatic animals produce nutrient-rich water. Land animals produce manures, so that your garden becomes a complete ecosystem.

TO FIND OUT MORE:

Cash from Your Garden: Roadside Farm Stands (by David W. Lynch, Garden Way, Charlotte, VT 05445, 1976) is a complete guide to setting up a roadside farm and garden market, from location to advertising and promotion, parking, merchandising and quality.

=49=
BOATRIDE/FERRY SERVICE

If you have the right waterside location, you can make money running boats. Tourists love paddling two-seat paddle boats. They also rent canoes, rowboats and motorboats for fun, sight-seeing and fishing.

A Chicago boat owner has begun commuting services for executives using the Chicago River.

Offer boat tours of metropolitan areas and of lakes and famous rivers. Offer speedboat rides for the thrill of it. Guide rafts through white water. Rent houseboats to vacationers looking for leisurely trips.

OTHER IDEAS:

Organize canoe trips.

PART III
RECYCLING

50
ANTIQUES

What's old is gold—that's what antique buyers and sellers are realizing more and more every day. And there's plenty of room for newcomers in the field.

Consider the aspects of trading in antiques: you can find antiques; sell them; buy them; deal in them; transport them from one market to another; fix, repair or refinish them to increase their value.

There are many places to find antiques. Hundreds of thousands of people all over the country have antiques stored in attics, basements and garages—but don't know it. Even on the most well-kept farms, old buildings are treasure troves of antiques. Decorators and antique buyers often look for horse collars, ancient scales, pickling crocks, corn huskers, small outmoded tools, plowshares, barbed wire, square nails, horseshoes, horseshoe nails, etc. Old radios, clocks, furniture, magazines, photographs, pictures, postcards, dolls, toy trains, sheet music, records, statuettes, posters, bottles, knickknacks, china, erotic art, books, maps, letters, insulators, candy tins and other old packaging, and canning jars are found in attics and basements on farms and in town.

How do you get to all these goodies? If you have a truck, you can become a scrap dealer, trucking farm and household scrap to recyclers. It may give you a chance to look inside homes, where you can offer to haul away "junk." There may be interesting and valuable items hidden in the junk and scrap.

Inspect garbage cans—people are constantly throwing out valuables. When an older person dies or moves to a retirement home or another city, get first dibs on what's left after the relatives are through. Offer free clean-out services to householders and landlords—you cart everything away. Help friends move— ask them to let you keep what they leave behind.

Scour the local dump for items which have already been thrown out (check local ordinances first, though, since many towns and cities ban dump sifting; in others, you'll have to pay the local dump manager a nominal fee for each item you remove from the dump).

You can also buy antiques. Smalltown shops are a possibility, since some smalltown shop owners don't know what antiques are worth and price some items far too high and others far too low (you want to buy the latter, of course). Remember, too, that most antique shop owners are willing to bargain.

House and farm auctions are also a good source for antiques —especially if another auction advertising antiques is taking place the same day or if a blizzard hits; other antique dealers are looking for bargains, too.

You might also try the antique shows, which are now set up at least once a year in towns and cities of almost every size. Other sources of goods are Salvation Army-type thrift shops, warehouse companies and demolition company lots.

Now that you've acquired all these antiques, how do you get rid of them? You could display them at a local antique show— or at a larger one where particular items may be more valuable. Or display them at flea markets. You may be able to convince a gift shop owner to display your antiques for sale on a consignment basis—you set the prices. You could open your own shop. You could invite antique dealers in to bid—or hold your own auction or antique show.

No matter how you obtain or get rid of your antiques, you'd better know plenty about them—or you'll get taken. And probably the best way to be knowledgeable about antiques is to specialize. There've been dozens of books written about each area of specialization, including collecting glass telephone pole insulators (and there are thousands of types, of varying value); collecting rare books; and collecting china. Those three areas represent but a tiny fraction of collectibles.

=51=
FURNITURE REFINISHER

Furniture refinishing is a task which requires time and tender loving care—for wood.

The process is really pretty simple. Strip finish from a piece of furniture with a liquid stripper (wear gloves) or tools, and then repair any damage to the wood itself and apply new stains and finishes.

Quite a number of people combine this with junk collecting. They find old furniture in garbage cans, farmers' dumps, second-hand stores, and household auctions. Then they redo it, and sell it at a tidy profit.

Some refinishers offer their services for hire—they refinish your furniture for you.

Other refinishers do reupholstery and/or recaning.

OTHER IDEAS:

Specialize in repairing and mending plastic and vinyl furniture.

52
FIREWOOD COLLECTOR

As the price of heating fuels rise, more and more people are turning to wood as a source of heat as well as of indoor comfort and beauty. Wood stoves and fireplaces are very popular, and the demand for firewood and wood-heating equipment has sky-rocketed.

The demand for wood-burning heaters is so great that some manufacturers have two-year waiting lists for delivery. Heaters can be constructed inexpensively from 55-gallon drums and heating pipe. Relatively sophisticated commercial units cost $200 to $500.

Since construction of wood heaters is a really low technology field, you don't have to be an electronics engineer to figure them out—you can probably build your own or build them for other people. Some people make a living installing them.

Supposedly men go out to the forest and "thin" it. In reality, they often chop trees unnecessarily. This is a tremendous waste, since so much wood is thrown out.

Wood from boxes, crates, construction and destruction of houses and buildings (think how much wood you could get from one house), carpentry and woodworking centers, private and commercial remodeling, unsightly billboards, trees chopped for disease or development, tree prunings, discarded trunks, unfixable furniture, discarded cable spools—the list is endless—all make good firewood. Newspapers can also be rolled into logs and used as firewood.

Collecting firewood can be profitable in other ways, too. If you find interesting pieces of wood, such as tree trunks, burls or furniture, you may be able to sell them or use them creatively. There are some "antique stores" in New York City that send out trucks looking for discarded fixable furniture, which often needs only cleaning or refinishing before it can be sold at ridiculously high prices. You may come across very salable lumber or plywood (also barn siding or weathered planks), old TV's, ornate molding (valuable to folks who restore old homes), lamps, almost anything.

If you decide to concentrate on firewood or paper logs, you can have a quite enjoyable and profitable business. You can build up a route of ecologically minded people. Signs in stores, in ecology publications and on bulletin boards will all attract customers. Just cut the wood to size and deliver it. People who have fireplaces will pay a premium for interestingly shaped pieces. One man, for example, paid an outrageous price for a cord of wooden table legs.

Softwoods are usually needed to start a fire because they catch easily; hardwoods are added later because they burn longer.

Before buying equipment, find out what you need; scour the area for wood to see what you come up with. You will need a truck or van and some tools. Power tools which run off your vehicle are very handy. You may need a power saw, large and small axes, crowbar, screwdrivers, pliers and wire cutters. Sometimes a lift or hoist is helpful.

Almost all wood and paper can be used for energy (running electric steam generators), newsprint (paper mills owned by lumber growers discourage recycling by keeping prices for used newsprint low), or for by-products like papier-mâché, mulch, and packing material, all of which are salable materials.

Collecting wood can be an interesting occupation. As you scour your community, you will develop a different understanding of what constitutes waste. You will also have the satisfaction of knowing that you personally have helped to solve the world's ecology and energy problems, lowering the profits of the energy corporations—even if only just a little.

OTHER IDEAS:

Cut down trees free in exchange for the wood. This especially helps senior citizens on fixed incomes, but anyone may take you up on your service.

Park departments sometimes offer cut trees free for the hauling.

TO FIND OUT MORE:

The Woodburners Encyclopedia: Wood as Energy (by Jay Shelton and Andrew B. Shapiro, Vermont Crossroads Press, Box 333, Waitsfield, VT 05673, 1977): If you get into wood, wood stoves or wood fireplaces in a big way, get this book. It's filled with information on energy, temperature, heat, etc., as well as a complete catalog of wood stoves, furnaces, splitting tools, etc.

=== 53 ===

HOUSE SITTER

What would you give to be able to live rent-free? Thousands are doing just that by house-sitting. Many move often, some as often as every week. All suffer changing addresses and phone numbers often. But they live rent-free—and rent seems to be, for most of us, our largest single expense. Some house sitters are even paid for their sitting.

To become a house sitter, you'll need some sort of permanent phone number—probably an answering service if you have no business number. You'll put the number on the dozens of notices announcing you are willing to house-sit, and you'll place the notices on bulletin boards all over the city you're living in. You also want to let all your local friends know you're available and willing to help them out by sitting with their houses—sitting for friends will help you put together the references strangers may ask you for.

Offer to take care of pets and plants. Have your references ready. You may be asked to take care of the lawn, garden, fruit trees, mail, newspapers, etc. Ideally, you'll find places which will be available to you for sitting for the same season, year after year.

OTHER IDEAS:

Be a houseparent or resident advisor in a college dorm or fraternity or sorority house.

Superintend an apartment building or house in exchange for rent. Duties will probably include keeping all apartments rented, and possibly building maintenance and/or lobby and hallway cleaning.

═══54═══

GARBAGE RECYCLER

"Garbage is only raw materials that we're too stupid to use."
—ARTHUR C. CLARKE

Ecology erupted as a mass movement in the late '60's, fueling drives to use less, have smaller families and recycle as much waste as possible. There was renewed interest in recycling centers for paper, metal and glass, and new centers started in communities of every size, from Ames, Iowa, to New York City. To many people, recycling paper was nothing new. My family has made a semiannual trip to the local paper company with a farm truck filled with newspapers and paper feed sacks ever since I was a small boy. But it took the ecology movement to trigger recycling on a large scale.

Recycling is a profitable business. The Boy Scouts sponsor paper drives, community groups run recycling centers, a growing number of privately owned companies are entering the industry, and local governments are salvaging waste. In most communities, though, there is plenty of room for one more recycling firm—the ones that exist just can't persuade everybody to store and recycle their trash, and the farther people have to transport the stuff, the less convinced they tend to be.

Paper is the easiest to collect and recycle. Prices paid for paper, which rose 1000 percent in 1973–74, plummeted during the next two years because paper companies were deluged with paper but make more money from virgin pulp, since they often own the pulp forests and logging companies. But many recyclers were making good profits even then. The demand exists, and you can supply it in three ways: establish a recycling center, a scheduled curbside paper pickup route, or a business waste pickup route.

In addition to newsprint, other paper waste materials you might consider recycling include computer punch cards and printout paper (both of which pay much better than newsprint), phone books, cardboard and corrugated cardboard, office wastepaper, and books and magazines. Some recyclers actually purchase corporate wastepaper or supermarket cardboard packaging materials to resell.

In Cincinnati, a man named Louis guarantees the destruction of sensitive corporate memos and correspondence. He bought a used paper shredder for $800. He charges $180 a ton to destroy. He turns around and sells the strip as packing material for $30 a ton. He handles two tons a week.

To set up recycling centers, try to get free space in parks and shopping centers, on university campuses and near stores. Some recyclers have paper pickup routes in residential neighborhoods. You should get cooperation from city government and university officials if you point out that you will be saving them trucking and landfill costs. Prove it and they might even give you free office space or even hire you as a consultant.

A rail transit system has the ideal setup for recycling. All subways and commuter railroads have platform cleanup crews. Suggest that they add a separate bin on each platform solely for recycling newspapers. Or four bins—for newspapers, glass, iron and aluminum. Newspapers, could bee transported by rail to a paper buyer, or to a power plant for burning. With little work on the part of the railroad, it gets a new revenue source—not to mention the publicity coup. Offer to run the recycling program for them.

If it rarely rains in your area, the enclosure you use for newsprint may consist of no more than chicken wire wrapped around four stakes. If it does rain, you might consider building a shed.

If you find yourself handling large quantities of paper, it might be worthwhile to invest in a paper baler. The 1500-pound bales sell for twice as much as loose paper, but the baler costs around $5000. (Lease-purchase plans are available.) Or arrange to use a baler in a box plant during evening hours when it's not in use. No matter what materials you recycle, you must have a truck or van to start.

Local manufacturers may also purchase your recycled newspapers. Millions of items are currently packaged in wrapping paper before boxing. In most cases, you can provide used newspapers at a lower price than tissue paper costs. Suggest it to manufacturers as both a money-saver and a public relations statement. One barbecue-grill manufacturer includes this statement on its assembly instruction sheet: "Recycled newspaper: to conserve newsprint we are using old newspaper which we have bought from local civic groups for the purpose of wrapping parts." The manufacturer might even get a puffy newspaper article out of the gimmick. Offer to write the press release; this, too, will get you more business.

Cans are another obvious recycling item, but check your community first. If most of the cans it uses are bimetallic, forget it; there's currently no profit in recycling them. On the other hand, if it uses a large percentage of all-aluminum or tin cans, collect only these and rake in the money. Beer and soft-drink distributors will often help you start your business.

Glass is recyclable too, but usually not very profitable; some urban areas may be an exception. It must be separated by color, can be dangerous, and should be crushed if you have to truck it very far. An electric glass crusher can be purchased for $200 and up, but consists of little more than a souped-up butter churn. Make it yourself.

Glass bottles and jars can be profitably recycled to local bottlers and for crafts. Cut and polished, they make unique glassware, vases, mugs, flowerpots, lamps, candleholders and terrariums.

Due to the oil shortage, plastics (produced from petroleum) are beginning to be recycled. If you have plastic processors in your area, check with them to see if they're buying. Use cardboard, plastic or metal barrels to collect glass, aluminum or plastic (but remember that metal barrels are very heavy).

Check with processors before recycling any materials. While there's a paper company near almost every town, the nearest aluminum, glass and plastic buyers may be hundreds of miles away. The farther you have to truck materials, the less profit you'll make.

Finally, seek out publicity. Ally yourself with community groups, local ecology groups and city government. Issue leaflets to tell people about recycling, and about your service and how to use it. And ask for (and ask the other organizations to ask for) free publicity in newspapers and on local TV and radio stations. After all, you're performing a service for the entire community.

TO FIND OUT MORE:

How to Start a Neighborhood Recycling Center (Ecology Center, 2179 Allstone Way, Berkeley, CA 94704) is a 30-page commonsense guide written and published by Berkeley's Ecology Center.

Organizations which can provide information on paper recycling include: U.S. Environmental Protection Agency, Office of Solid Waste Management Programs, Washington, DC 20460; National Center for Resource Recovery, Inc., 1211 Connecticut Ave., N.W., Washington, DC 20036; Forest Products Laboratory, U.S. Dept. of Agriculture, P.O. Box 5130, Madison, WI 53705; National Association of Recycling Industries, Inc., 330 Madison Ave., New York, NY 10017; and American Paper Institute, 260 Madison Ave., New York, NY 10016.

The Environmental Action Coalition (235 E. 49 St., New York, NY 10017) has valuable tips on setting up recycling centers.

The townspeople of Nottingham, New York, population 1200, constructed an inexpensive newspaper baler and improvised other low-cost equipment for their paper, glass and metal recycling center. They welcome duplication. Write: Recycle-Conservation, Inc., Box 276, Kittery, ME 03904.

Among aluminum-can buyers are Reynolds (Richmond, VA 23261; toll-free 800-243-6000 or in CT, 800-882-6500), Coors (PR Dept 802, Golden, CO 80401), and Kaiser (415-271-3469 in the San Francisco area).

55
NEWSPAPER CLIPPING AGENCY

Two West Coast media freaks decided to turn their obsession for knowing the news into dollars. They opened a clipping service. These days, they read every newspaper from ten western states —with scissors. They charge their customers about $25 per month for the first 100 clippings, and 3¢ per clipping after that. Subjects their customers have chosen to have clipped include drugs, small businesses and environmental issues.

They affix a slip of paper printed with the name of the publication to the top of each clipping and write in the date.

In Montreal, a man who says he's disabled clips the local newspaper and sends copies of articles to the people they're about, with a card explaining his service and who he is, and requesting a donation.

OTHER IDEAS:

Some organizations will pay for a list of the names and addresses of all births within an area or region; others, all the deaths; still others, all persons getting married, or moving to an area, or graduating, or buying new homes. Call or write mail-order firms to learn their needs and prices.

Combine with freelance writing: Send local paper clippings to trade journals—a local feature on a bakery to a bakers' magazine, for example. Include a stamped, self-addressed envelope. If you get it back, try the next bakers' magazine.

Public relations departments of large companies and corporations are always interested in getting copies of local articles about themselves, their corporate officers and managerial staffs, and their products. Public figures and politicians, too, are interested in news about themselves. They undoubtedly see syndicated stories (from AP, UPI, etc.), so stick to strictly local stories. Send them a postcard on which you've rubber-stamped something like, "A story about _____ appeared in _____ on _____. Send $4 for _____ copies of this story." Fill in the blanks with name of subject, name of publication in which the story appeared, date, what you're offering. And send the article if and when they send the money.

═══56═══
JUNK COLLECTOR

American business thrives on waste. It created the concepts of planned obsolescence, New-Improved-Bigger-and-Better and Buy-Now-and-Save. It fosters the illusion that resources are unlimited and can be squandered and wasted. In its drive for profits, it brainwashes consumers to believe that new goods mean happiness.

Every day millions of still usable, fixable or valuable goods are thrown out, discarded, to become part of the junkpile of solid waste that typifies the real corporate image.

So much is thrown out that people in an "undeveloped" country the size of the U.S. could probably live on it. One study shows that 15 percent of the food Americans buy winds up in the garbage pail. Consumers are taught to buy new TV's, radios, toasters and other small appliances, washers, dryers and refrigerators, rather than repairing the old, which have been designed to wear out. They wear clothing only as long as it is stylish, and constantly replace perfectly usable furniture and cars.

Industry also discards salvageable goods. Companies chuck items that are slightly damaged, that are made "obsolete" by "more efficient" tools, or which still have usable components. Industrial concerns often dump goods that have salvage value.

Collecting junk takes little or no start-up capital. You'll need a vehicle and an eagle eye. There are salvageable goods everywhere. Streets are lined with furniture, clothing, and abandoned cars, and dumpsters are filled with "junk." (I furnished my San Francisco apartment from the "street" and dumpsters. I found an unused pink Bigelow rug and padding, chests, tables, lamps, a desk, drapes, curtains, the frame for my bed, plants, pots, pans and accessories.)

Once you begin to look, you will see more stuff than you would ever have believed was there. And somebody undoubtedly will buy what you find.

A. J. Weberman is a "garbologist." He lives in New York City, the junk-collecting capital of the United States. He practically wrote the book on dumpstering. First he furnished his apartment out of Manhattan dumpsters. Then, while studying Bob Dylan, he decided to examine his subject's garbage, discovering a new means of understanding the rich and powerful. Eventually he wrote an article for *Esquire* magazine revealing the contents of famous people's garbage. A. J. looks everywhere. He keeps his eyes open for treasures wherever they might appear, and has found useful goods all over the city—in garbage cans and dumpsters, abandoned buildings, empty lots—even on the subway.

Ed collects old thermometer beverage signs ("It's 80—Time for Nehi"). On trips to rural areas he finds or buys them for nominal sums, then sells them at a Sausalito flea market for $30 each.

Maraya has always been interested in dolls. She buys broken ones from the Salvation Army "as is" shop, repairs them, and sells them at the flea market. She has built up a customer list and phones her regulars whenever she has a rare find to sell. Other people at the "as is" shop specialize in broken TV's, toasters, knives and toys.

Stephen bought a piece of land in Maui, Hawaii. Since building materials are so expensive there, he decided to use only salvaged goods. He was surprised when he gathered all the glass, wood, electrical equipment and plumbing supplies in less than two weeks. He now lives in a "recycled" house with windmill and solar heating.

There is a dumpster near Los Angeles which a "straight thrift shop" uses to dump its unsalable clothing. Susan checks it daily for antique dresses, velvet, satin and lace. She repairs some garments and sells them to a fashion boutique. She sells the cloth "as is" at the flea market.

In New Haven, there is an electronics company which "dumpsters" malfunctioning components. Each piece it throws out has four silver welds and a thin gold wire. Johann retrieves about 2000 of these each week, and with fine pliers he plucks out the gold and silver. He sells three ounces of gold a week.

Roger lives near Flagstaff, Arizona. When he left Baltimore, he decided that he wanted to get involved in recycling. Each day he picks up the table scraps and organic wastes from several restaurants and food stores. He feeds some of it to his chickens and the rest goes directly into a compost pile. Anything the chickens don't eat remains on the ground. He shovels chicken droppings and leftover garbage from the coop once a month and adds it to the compost heaps, which produce a ton of compost a week. As each pile cools he adds worms, which quickly multiply and fertilize the compost. He sells eggs, worms, and compost with worms. He does not pay for any raw material (the restaurants and food stores are happy to give him their waste instead of paying to have it removed), but makes over $300 a week.

OTHER IDEAS:

If you're really good at junk collecting, teach a class in it or lecture to groups.

Dismantle and salvage used building materials.

TO FIND OUT MORE:

How I Turn Junk into Fun and Profit (as told to Uncle Milton by Sari; Wilshire Book Co., 12015 Sherman Rd., N. Hollywood, CA 91605, 1974) is the delightful story of a suburban housewife who turned junk first into furniture and then into club bookings, college classes, a book, and a half-hour TV show. Transformations include a chicken coop into a bookcase and an old shoe plus a plastic detergent bottle into a highbutton-shoe vase. Sari says, "It's not really junk. It's just something that needs an idea!"

The Getting Game (by George Daniels, Harper & Row, 1974) is a great book on how to live better on less. Not really a how-to, it's an account of how the author and his family lived—built their own luxury car, owned several homes dirt-cheap, etc. Fascinating reading.

═ 57 ═
USED BOOK/
RECORD EXCHANGE

Reading books and listening to records are enjoyable and fascinating forms of entertainment for most folks. If you're one of them, why not open a used book or record exchange for your fellow book and record lovers? It can be fun, entertaining and profitable.

A used book exchange could be started in the living room or porch of your home. Start it with that pile of books you've had lying around the house or stacked on bookshelves for years. Pull out the ones you'll never read again. Add to your own stock by investing in paperbacks—you should be able to get them for a dime apiece—people just like yourself have accumulated books and would just as soon have cash for them. You might advertise in the classifieds that you'll pay cash for books.

When you've got a couple of thousand titles, arrange the books by type on shelves or tables. Put up a sign in front of your house (providing local ordinances allow it) to offer, "Bring in two books, get one free" or "Book Exchange: Books 25¢ to $1.00." Use the same slogans on the radio or in the classifieds in the local daily, college paper or alternative paper.

With the two-for-one idea, you should be able to increase your stock easily. And most avid readers won't have as many books to trade in as they want to take home—so they'll buy the rest from you. You could specialize in college texts, science fiction, westerns, mysteries or gothics. The record exchange works basically the same way, but you must be careful to examine both sides of each disc for scratches.

Once you've got the book exchange going well, you could move it to a well-located store. Install Coke machines, pinball machines, electronic games, magazine racks, reading tables, cigarettes, candy, greeting cards, rolling papers, snacks (or snack machines), and gifts. Keep your exchange well lit and open evenings; use your imagination for adding sidelines to the business, and you're likely to do very well indeed.

OTHER IDEAS:

In Meyersville, New Jersey, Archie Stiles opened a toy resale shop. And Toy-Go-Round in Berkeley, California, will sell your outgrown toys on a commission basis for 50 percent.

Open a used comics and comix store.

TO FIND OUT MORE:

How to Run a Paperback Bookshop (ed. by Sidney Gross and Phyllis B. Steckler, R. R. Bowker, 1965) offers some good hints on running bookstores—locations, merchandising, display, etc.

PART IV
LABOR

58
PLASTERER/
WALLPAPERER/PAINTER

There comes a time in the life of every home or apartment dweller when the walls begin to close in from ugliness—when the psychological lifespan of the last paint job has expired.

Many of us do our own plastering and plaster repairs, our own wallpapering, our own painting. Others have it done by professionals.

If you're a do-it-yourselfer, you've undoubtedly already had some experience with plastering, wallpapering and painting. If you enjoy it, you can make money doing it for a living. Thousands of college students put themselves through school each year by painting the exteriors and interiors of houses during the summer. But do it right. Study the skills and get them down; though most people don't realize it, there's more to a paint job than just two new coats. Practice, preferably on your own pad. Then do it.

OTHER IDEAS:

Install wood paneling.

Specialize in removing wallpaper and paneling.

Specialize in bathrooms. Get to know wall tile and waterproof paints, panelings and coatings.

Paint rusty TV antenna towers with rustproof aluminum paint

(use a painting glove). Sell the service door-to-door to home-owners.

Bid on contracts to paint local government buildings.

Paint curbs with house numbers—paint a rectangle of white on the curb and spray-paint stencils of the numbers on top.

TO FIND OUT MORE:

Paneling, Painting and Wallpapering (by the Editors of Sunset Books, Lane Publishing, Menlo Park, CA, 1976) is both a full-color creative idea book and a how-to for each of the techniques involved.

How to Do Your Own Painting and Wallpapering (by Jackson Hand, Popular Science/Harper & Row, 1976): There's more to painting than you think, as a quick read through this book will show; a slow read will teach you even more.

The Wall Book (by Stanley Schuler, M. Evans, 1974) gives a solid base of introductory information on walls, wall-paper, coverings, gypsum board, plaster, paneling, plywood, mirrors, tile, masonry, luminous walls, and much more.

The Painting and Decorating Contractors of America (7223 Lee Highway, Falls Church, VA 22046) is a trade group for painting, decorating and drywall contractors. It wants to make the public aware that "Professional Painting Pays." It publishes a monthly journal, business management manuals, an estimating guide, and a textbook and manual. It holds workshops.

Remodeling Rooms: Walls, Floors, Ceilings (by Richard Day, Arco, 1969) is both an excellent idea book and a how-to for floor tile, wallpapering, paneling, tiling, and more.

59
FLOOR REFINISHER

Floor refinishing is the kind of skill that is so in demand that you could take your service door-to-door in many suburbs and continually find jobs. (Before you go door-to-door selling any service or product, though, be sure it's legal—some communities have adopted "Green River Ordinances" which prohibit door-to-door sales).

Floor refinishers strip, stain and wax wood floors, and shampoo and scrub carpets. They do the kinds of jobs that many people hate to do themselves. Try it—and if you like it you'll find an abundance of jobs awaiting you.

OTHER IDEAS:

Start a carpet steam-cleaning service.

Lay tile, linoleum or carpet, or repair wooden floors.

Set up a parquet design studio.

Customize floors with murals, designs or collages decoupaged to the floor or using inlays.

60

BASEMENT/ GARAGE/ATTIC CLEANER

There's intrigue in cleaning other people's basements, garages and attics, even when there's nothing but drudgery involved in doing our own; almost all of us at one time or another have wished we could clean out Aunt Agnes' attic or brother Bob's basement. We know that what they consider junk is just what we've been looking for all these years. If you enjoy cleaning out someone else's storage spaces, do it for a living.

Charge by the hour—or make an estimate for the job. Some of the "junk" your clients have asked you to throw out will be immediately salable, providing a second source of income from this work. Some storage-space cleaners, particularly in urban areas, approach the job by offering to clean junk rooms free to carry off all the flea-marketables they like.

If you live in a rural area, you may want to extend your services to include barns, pumphouses, machine sheds and truck garages.

OTHER IDEAS:

Hire out to clean debris from yards and lots.

Offer a cleaning service for rental firms, real-estate agencies and management companies. Clean up spaces when commercial or industrial firms move, or when new tenants move in.

Your service may also include repairs and painting.

61
BRICKLAYER

Laying bricks requires careful work. Learn the skills involved by apprenticing with a bricklayer. Or begin with concrete block or brick walls and fences and work your way up to indoor fireplaces, foundations (check local building codes—they're outlawed in earthquake zones), and homes.

Your state or locality may require certification, licensing or a union card for some of these jobs.

OTHER IDEAS:

Specialize in outdoor patios and outdoor brick fireplaces.
Construct brick or stone sidewalks and paths.
Do metalwork.
Install insulation.
Work with fiberglass.
Pour concrete and cement.

TO FIND OUT MORE:

Bricklaying Simplified (by Donald R. Brann, Directions Simplified, Briarcliff Manor. NY 10510) will teach you a great deal about laying brick with its easy-to-study, well-illustrated style.

Concrete, Masonry and Brickwork: A Practical Handbook for the Home Owner and Small Builder (by the U.S. Dept. of the Army, Dover, 1975) is an invaluable reference book if you're laying brick, block or concrete for pay.

How to Work with Masonry and Concrete (by John Burton Brimer, Theodore Audel & Co., Howard W. Sams, 1971) covers bricks, block, rock and concrete; it could be better, but offers good basic information.

How to Plan and Build Fireplaces (by the Editors of Sunset Books, Lane Books, Menlo Park, CA, 1973) is a well-illustrated guide to hundreds of fireplaces and how to build or install them.

═══62═══
LAUNDRY/IRONING SERVICE

Millions find doing laundry and ironing drudgery. If you're one of them, you need read no further in this chapter. On the other hand, if you find laundering and ironing fun, do it.

Start with a washer, a dryer and a clothesline—buy a used heavy-duty washer and gas-heated dryer. Then advertise, especially on bulletin boards (even better, on bulletin boards in Laundromats, if you can get away with it). Those millions who hate laundering and ironing—many, many of them single professional people—will come flocking to your door. And if the price is right, they'll come back again and again.

You might do even better if you try a laundry pickup and delivery route in your neighborhood.

63
MESSENGER SERVICE

If you've ever worked for a business, you know that all too often, there are more things to go "fer" than there are gofers to fetch them.

Visit with the office managers and business people in your neighborhood, leaving your card with each one; urge them to call on you when they need something sent out or picked up.

In major cities, messenger services use young bicyclists with small CB radios to pick up and deliver messages and small packages. They pay the messengers by the job. One innovative messenger bought himself a moped and increased his volume considerably.

Messenger services also use motorcyclists, especially on trips to and from airports and between twin cities such as Oakland and San Francisco.

One courier service delivers confidential memoranda between offices and corporations in major cities. It finds sending material by courier cheaper than paying air freight. The couriers fly free. They are usually young people who have heard of the service by word-of-mouth.

OTHER IDEAS:

Offer a once- or twice-daily delivery service between nearby cities or towns—for instance, between Waterloo, Des Moines and Cedar Rapids. A round trip between these cities takes about

5½ hours. With time for pickups, the trip would take about eight hours. If you had once-a-day service, you could guarantee delivery within 24 hours.

Run a delivery service for local stores. Pharmacies, food stores, and clothing and specialty shops all could use a reliable delivery service.

64
SNOW SHOVELER/ ODD JOBBER/ HANDYPERSON

Home owners and apartment dwellers alike are often on the lookout for those good at doing jobs with their hands and muscles.

Jobs include: washing windows; installing window grates, gates and other security devices; shoveling snow; raking leaves; mowing lawns; washing windows; washing cars; and providing extra hands for moving, painting, and other household chores.

An Oakland, California, man placed one classified ad as a skilled handyman in his local newspaper and had more requests for his services than he could handle. A New York City woman has a general house repair shop. She frequently changes door locks for new apartment tenants, installs window grates, and puts up decorative shutters and plant hangers.

Don't be afraid to ask reasonable rates for your services. This know-how is a valuable skill. People are willing to pay for good work.

65
BULLETIN BOARD
AD SERVICE

Bulletin-board advertising can be cheap and effective. But in metropolitan areas, it can be difficult to discover and tedious to poster every good bulletin board in town.

Naturally enough, that has been the starting point for companies in several cities. The Thumbtack Bugle, a poster distribution service in San Francisco and Berkeley, is typical.

The Bugle charges less than $20 to tack up letter-size or smaller posters and flyers on over 100 good bulletin boards in either Berkeley or San Francisco. The flyers are distributed twice a month (deadlines are the 15th and the 30th), 20 different flyers at a time, by motorcycle. The Bugle advertises its service on bulletin boards (where else?). "We guarantee city-wide bulletin board distribution for a fraction of what it would cost you," reads the Bugle's own flyer.

OTHER IDEAS:

Start a bound-leaflet service. Deliver books of 50 different leaflets of events, sales, courses and public notices to stores and restaurants, where they are placed on counters, as well as in reception areas, waiting rooms and dormitory parlors. Guarantee delivery and replace the book each week.

═66═
THIRD-CLASS
MAIL SERVICE

Businesses pay plenty for both newspaper and circular advertising. You can offer them a third alternative.

Pick out specific neighborhoods. Know their demographics—where the singles live, where older people live, where the middle class lives, where the upper class lives, where married people live. In large cities, identifiable groups of people like these often live together in specific areas.

Approach businesses. Find out whom their advertising is aimed toward. Then offer to reach that clientele more directly and less expensively. Offer cheaper rates than the postal service (the way rates are going, that is no longer very difficult). Convince ten different stores to sign up for the same neighborhood. Then make up packets of ten flyers, one flyer from each store, and deliver them door to door.

OTHER IDEAS:

Deliver samples from manufacturers in packets.

Since mailboxes are considered government property and it's illegal for anyone else to use them, some people put packets into plastic bags designed with holes big enough to hang the bags on doorknobs.

Deliver bills or supermarket flyers, magazines or newspapers.

67
TRUCKER/HAULER/ DELIVERY SERVICE

A friend of mine who lives in New York City bought an old Dodge van for $300 and started a small trucking/hauling service. He placed an advertisement in the *Village Voice*, a weekly paper, and placed notices in grocery stores and Laundromats. He speaks a little Spanish, so he wrote notices in both English and Spanish. He charges $8 an hour with a two-hour minimum. Since his first month, he has had to turn away work.

He is very reliable and gets word-of-mouth recommendations. Several stores use his service every week to make deliveries, and he hauls supplies for a small manufacturer.

He says that he tries to limit his service to 25 hours a week, but he is in such demand that he lets a friend do some jobs. He is a strong person, but he sometimes needs a helper, usually his friend, for whom he charges an additional $4 an hour.

"I enjoy hauling because I make my own hours, meet nice people, make good money, and I'm not in some uptown office. I was an order clerk for a year and a half and I hated it. Now I like what I do. Also, I get plenty of exercise hauling, and I keep in shape."

People who prefer to truck in the evening are often in demand by people who work during the day, so make your own schedule.

To start, you need a van or truck, some moving blankets, publicity or advertising, and a telephone-answering service or machine.

You might begin by charging less than most other area movers charge. Then raise your prices when you're getting more customers than you want to handle.

Since many movers won't take customers who must move furniture up or down stairs, you can attract customers by advertising that you will.

TO FIND OUT MORE:

The Family Guide to Successful Moving (by Carl Warmington, Association Press, 1968) and *Do-It-Yourself Moving* (by George Sullivan, Collier, 1973) are written for the consumer—which makes them musts for reading if you're the mover. You may want to give your customers the kind of advice found here —they'll thank you for it. Buy copies of the books wholesale, and sell them to customers.

=68=
JANITOR SERVICE

Janitoring is for people who enjoy cleaning. Janitors often get to work alone or with a compatible group of people in quiet, empty buildings; some claim it's good for the soul.

To start a janitor service, you'll need dust mops, wet mops, and mop buckets or floor-washing machines. You'll also need sponges and cleansers, detergents and waxes.

Sell your service to commercial and industrial concerns, small business offices and health clubs; leave your card even if they don't seem interested—urge them to keep you in mind should their present janitors not work out.

Getting your janitor service going will probably take time. So once contracts are signed, provide good service and keep in touch with your clients. Ask them if there's any way you can improve the way their buildings are cleaned.

Some people earn a living as window washers. Most washers service stores with large front windows. But some window cleaners service office or residential buildings.

OTHER IDEAS:

After working each job for several weeks to understand its requirements, hire others to do it, and divide the fee with them. Then devote your time again to selling jobs.

Become a house cleaner. Work on a weekly or semi-weekly basis, or come after parties or for seasonal cleanups (spring cleaning). Demand decent pay. Housecleaners in San Francisco make up to $6 an hour.

TO FIND OUT MORE:

Building Service Contractors Association International (1750 Old Meadow Rd., McLean, VA 22101) is an organization of professional cleaning and maintenance contractors. It publishes a monthly bulletin and trade materials such as "Marketing Building Services," "Bidding and Estimating" and "Model Proposal Guidebook," free to members. It holds seminars and confabs, and provides other services. It is expensive—$250 per year plus initiation for companies grossing less than $500,000— which gives you an idea of its membership.

The American Institute of Maintenance (P.O. Box 2068, Glendale, CA 91209) is a membership organization for persons in "cleaning maintenance and management." It publishes a bimonthly *Cleaning Management* magazine and a bimonthly *Custodial Operations* bulletin, offers various technical books like

Floor Care Guide and *Handy Maintenance Tips*, and offers home-study courses.

Professional Cleaning and Building Maintenance: How to Organize a Money-Saving Service Business or a Department for Floor and Building Cleaning (by Bill Clark, Exposition Press, NY, 1960) is a complete guide to the business, including equipping a truck, sales presentations, floor maintenance, washing, and skilled specialties.

Industrial Housekeeping: Its Technology and Technique (by Edwin B. Feldman, Macmillan, 1963) offers good advice for cleaning and maintenance—though written for the factory owner, not the factory cleaner.

═══ 69 ═══
NEWSPAPER/
MAGAZINE DELIVERY SERVICE

Post office delivery of newspapers and magazines gets less reliable and more expensive each year, so local newspapers often have their own delivery routes. But regional and national newspapers and magazines have difficulty setting up delivery services.

If you enjoy working with kids and young teens, this may be a good business for you. Is there significant demand in your town or on a nearby college campus for the *New York Times*, the *Denver Post*, the *Wall Street Journal*, or the *Des Moines Register*? How about *Rolling Stone, Playboy, Time, Newsweek, High Times, Yipster Times* or books from specialty publishers?

Make arrangements with newspaper and magazine publishers

to distribute their periodicals in your area. Divide the area into routes and have the publishers print the route numbers on the periodicals' labels; charge a fee for each journal delivered and for new subscriptions your carriers write. Split the fees with the carriers; the carriers will get most of the fee, but you will receive a small percentage for each delivery. You may spur new subscription sales by giving prizes to carriers who bring in new subscriptions.

Let your customers know you are doing their deliveries and give them your phone number so they have someone to call to complain if a periodical doesn't show up on time. Be sure to be prompt with your deliveries. You may also want to deliver advertising brochures for local businesses.

Another method of distributing newspapers and magazines is through coin-operated news boxes. These can be purchased used for as little as $20 each. A Berkeley, California, distributor of *Yipster Times* put five coin boxes on the streets of Berkeley. He checked them once a week (it takes an hour), was rarely ripped off, and sold a hundred or more a week (making $15).

70
SHINGLER/GLAZIER/ PLUMBER/ELECTRICIAN

According to home owners, there is a shortage of skilled craftspeople who make house calls. Most skilled people work for shops, which are taking on more contract work building or reconstructing on a mass-production level. Fewer shops do individual work such as fixing shingles, replacing window glass, snaking out a drain pipe, or wiring a clothes dryer.

In many states, you have to be licensed to do this kind of work.

71
SERVICES FOR THE HANDICAPPED

Many handicapped people demand independence; they do day-to-day tasks by themselves.

But some Americans are too handicapped for total independence. Quadriplegics, for example, may require transportation as well as help with chores, feeding, cooking, and even bowel movements.

In Berkeley, California, the Center for Independent Living (CIL) helps handicapped persons learn to cope and deal with their needs and the world. It links the handicapped with persons who want to be their helpers. Some helpers are paid a salary; others may get free room and board, plus a fee.

You can sometimes find situations to help handicapped persons through classified ads. Many other handicapped persons seek help through agencies like CIL, as well as through local, state and federal agencies.

This can be both an emotionally draining and an emotionally rewarding occupation.

PART V
VENDING

72

FLOWER ARRANGER/ FLOWER STAND

Americans love flowers. They almost always use them on the three most important occasions in their lives—their births, marriages and deaths. Sweethearts give each other flowers. Employees give their employers flowers. And the sanctuaries of most churches are lined with flowers every Sunday.

There are professionals who arrange all those flowers, and you can be one of them.

A woman in Iowa started her flower business in her garage. Despite the fact that her home was located on a gravel road in the middle of farm country, her neighbors trooped in from miles around to buy flowers from her. She is always willing to sit down with a customer to plan all the flowers for a wedding. And when the wedding day comes, she arrives with flowers, vases, arrangements, hair pieces, baskets, stands and anything else needed in plenty of time to get everything set up long before the ceremony begins. Promptness and price are two reasons why she always has more business than she needs and why she's had to build additions to her garage to house her business.

A New York man sells flowers and arrangements at Pennsylvania Station. He'll sell flowers singly or wrap them into a quick corsage on a moment's notice. His location in one of the entrances to the busy train station brings him plenty of business at any hour.

Toby Florer of Dallas, Texas, always wanted to be a clown. Now he's selling flowers—in white-painted face and clown's outfit on street corners. On a good day he sells over a hundred dollars' worth of flowers—due in part to his antics and costume.

Flower vendors still traverse the streets of New York with pushcarts loaded with flowers. The followers of Reverend Moon have financed his conservative political movement by selling flowers in cities throughout the U.S. Some persons sell flowers only on special days—green-tinted carnations on St. Patrick's Day, for example. Others set up flower stands at trade shows and flea markets, bus stations and busy street corners.

OTHER IDEAS:

Arrange dried flowers.

Develop a clientele which has a "permanent order" for flowers to be delivered weekly.

Sell corsages to groups and institutions for special events, such as proms or employee appreciation days.

TO FIND OUT MORE:

Flower News (tabloid; 549 W. Randolph St., Chicago, IL 60606) emphasizes that it is a trade publication for the floral industry. If you're seriously contemplating the flower business, it looks worthwhile. Once a month it runs a special issue for growers and nursery folks.

The Society of American Florists (901 N. Washington St., Alexandria, VA 22314) provides members with how-to information on marketing methods, employee relations, tax questions and federal regulations. It publishes a monthly newspaper, "The American Florist—Dateline Washington."

The Retail Florist Business (by Peter B. Pfahl, The Interstate, 19-27 N. Jackson St., Danville, IL 61832,1977) is a textbook on this subject, and delves into such topics as window display, starting costs, interior design and layout, management, design schools, buying, markup, advertising and publicity, selling, tricks of the trade (very useful), wiring flowers, accounting, and entire sections of flower-arranging design and special uses for flowers.

And, of course, there's a flower-arranging book (or a dozen) for every taste.

73
FOOD VENDOR

Last year I went to the Talent, Oregon, Harvest Festival. It's a laid-back local fair held each August. I was with two kids and they were thirsty and hungry as soon as we got there. One concessionaire dressed in a striped hat and red tie was squeezing lemons, mixing the juice with sugar, ice and water, and selling it as fresh-squeezed lemonade.

I bought three, one medium at 50¢ and two small ones at 35¢. It sure was thirst-quenching, and he had a line of people for five hours. He usually sets up five miles from Talent, in the lobby of a store in central Ashland. It's a busy area and he does very well on hot, sunny days.

Other concessionaires at the Harvest Festival were the Fire Department's Women's Auxiliary selling barbecued beef on a bun; the Lions Club selling hamburgers; a commune selling chow mein and brown rice; and the Women's Club selling corn dogs. There were also stands for popcorn and batter-fried chicken. Most of the concessionaries set up only one or two times a season.

John Fogarty used to work in the Youngstown Steel Mill in Ohio. When he was laid off, he bought an old milk van and converted it into a mobile canteen. He and his wife developed a regular coffee-break route which services four different factories. Each morning they greet his former co-workers at the factory gate with coffee and pastries.

Food vending can be an enjoyable way to earn a living. You meet all kinds of people, are outdoors a lot and are independent. With ingenuity you can create an extremely profitable business. Thousands of people vend ready-to-eat food from pushcarts, stands and trucks. In major cities, people sell hot dogs, pretzels, fruit, sodas, and ethnic foods from pushcarts on the streets. And another kind of cart is pushed up and down office-building hallways during coffee breaks. Some colleges and resort areas allow stands or rent out concessions.

There are vendors who follow fairs, traveling circuses, rodeos and other shows. Other people sell at events like rallies, outdoor rock concerts, and happenings. In New York City, people sell Italian food at Catholic Church-sponsored street festivals. They pay rent for their space on the street to the church committee. They have movable stands and tow them from festival to festival.

There are pushcarts and stands which are made for handling food. They are usually expensive, so some people make their own. Heated ones are usually fueled by charcoal or bottled gas. You can buy food and supplies from food wholesalers and restaurant-supply houses.

Fast-food ideas include burritos, souvlaki, specialty hot dogs and hamburgers, and shish kebab.

Vegetarian fast foods include falafel, shrimp rolls, organic pizza, and stuffed grape leaves.

Most areas require licensing and certification for food vendors and equipment. Regulations vary from locality to locality, but they are usually enforced stringently. Before setting up, find out what you must do to meet these requirements.

74

MEMENTOES— MAKE THEM AND SELL THEM

When the blizzards hit Buffalo, New York, in 1977, residents were driven indoors by the worst winter weather in 107 years. Some residents used the indoor confinement to good advantage, producing dozens of ideas for mementoes.

Big sellers included T-shirts, jewelry, postcards, and dollar (retail) "Certificates of Survival" from the "Blizzard of '77." There was a 14-karat-gold snow-shovel charm priced at $50. Other products which sold well included $8 sweatshirts, $4 T-shirts (saying "I survived the Blizzard of '77"), $8.50 sterling silver snowflakes, and $2.50 mugs emblazoned with details of the storm. Buffalo photographer Peter Levin sold more than 3500 postcards, at 25¢ each, of photos around his neighborhood.

America's Bicentennial was a banner year for memento producers. Thousands of products were made and sold during the Bicentennial celebration.

Queen Elizabeth's Silver Jubilee—her 25th year of reign over England, in 1977—brought memento producers scrambling for profits, too. And Jimmy Carter's election brought forth a Plains, Georgia, coloring book, a peanut-shaped fishing lure, and even a Jimmy Carter peanut roach clip.

Mementoes and souvenirs can be linked to almost any place or time. Is your town, or one near you, celebrating an event or historical anniversary, or has it overcome some calamity? Is there some attraction nearby to memorialize on a T-shirt? Or some dirty bit of history your town would like to remember—or forget? Each has the makings of a good subject for your memento company.

OTHER IDEAS:

Political and cultural movements often finance their events through the sale of T-shirts, buttons and other mementoes of demonstrations or causes. In France, for example, inch-high guillotine pendants sell well to opponents of capital punishment.

Sell mementoes of past events. For instance, a Youth International Party "Eat the Rich" T-shirt from 1972 in fair condition recently sold for $12, and old 25¢ Amorphia (marijuana legalization organization, early '70's) buttons sell for 75¢ and more these days.

Spinoffs from movies and personalities are often licensed. Everyone remembers the Davy Crockett spinoffs, ranging from raccoon caps to lunchboxes. Licensing royalties from *Star Wars* made Twentieth Century-Fox an estimated $5,000,000 gross in 1977, and over 75,000 Farrah Fawcett-Majors posters sold in one week. You, too, may have a licenseable image. Or perhaps you know someone who does and can make or help make the licensing arrangements.

Mickey Mouse and Spiro Agnew watches have also been popular. Custom watchfaces can be "manufactured," using self-stick decals and stock watches.

Have sew-on patches custom-made for clubs, conventions, etc.

TO FIND OUT MORE:

A.T. Patch Co., RFD 1, Littleton, NH 03561 makes sew-on patches to order.

75

CATERER/COOK/ SANDWICH SERVICE

Every weeknight at Iowa State University, a dozen young men and women fill milk carriers with various kinds of sandwiches and chips, hardboiled eggs, milk, candy and other goodies. Then they begin their routes; they enter the front parlors of dorms, fraternities, and sororities during the traditional evening study hours, belting out a stomach-curdling cry, "Sandwich Man."

A competing service also thrives. It employs people to sell submarine sandwiches to the same fraternity/sorority/dorm crowd.

Both sandwich services are successful because the salespeople develop routes, and arrive dependably at about the same time every night, week after week.

There are wholesale sandwich services. They sell to groceries, delis, quick-stop shops and snack trucks, a tray at a time for morning and lunchtime sales. Another caterer sells a hundred sack lunches at a time to fraternities and sororities on football game days.

A Riverton, Wyoming, woman has built herself a good business catering weddings, showers and parties. She prepares incredible arrays of food and drink: trays of hors d'oeuvres, delicate finger sandwiches with her own spreads, homemade mints, homemade doughnuts, finger-licking homemade pastries, and more. She always arrives early, dressed in a French waitress outfit, to set up and make sure the food end of things moves smoothly. Needless to say, her catering service is in demand.

A specialist, Saul, the Omelette Man, is the rage of New York's nouveau-riche party scene. Saul comes dressed in tails, toting butane torches for burners, pans, and all the ingredients for the several different omelettes he will offer guests during the evening.

Be sure to check and follow local and state health codes.

OTHER IDEAS:

Offer your specialty—salads, soufflés, box lunches, casseroles or snack trays for parties, picnics or other events. You could also direct the party, not only serving food but also providing the servers, place cards, entertainment, decoration and cleanup.

Specialize in ethnic, organic or exotic foods for sale in stores and groceries.

Specialize in special diet foods, such as salt-free or fat-free dishes. You could develop a delivery route for your special cooking, either steaming hot or packaged in portion-sized containers or plastic bags, frozen for use as a convenience food. People on special diets would consider you a godsend.

Set up a take-out-and-delivery meal center featuring Italian, American, Oriental or Mexican food.

Make up and send care packages and food and fruit baskets to kids in college. Solicit parents to pay. Or provide birthday cakes or cookies on contract.

Provide school lunches—well-balanced meals, of course—for parents to send to school with their kids. Do it well enough and word will spread from kid to kid until they're all demanding that their parents buy your lunches.

Be a bartender at parties and cater the booze.

TO FIND OUT MORE:

Making Money in Your Kitchen: Over 1600 Products that Women Can Make (by Helen Stone Hovey, Wilfred Funk, 1953) is a useful and complete guide on the subject.

76

CRAFTSPERSON/ STREET ARTIST

Many people have found the answer to their money problems in crafts. In the past few years, thousands of craft shows have started all over the country. In San Francisco, New York, Boston, and other cities, craftspeople, or street artists, sell their work on the street every day (weather permitting).

Crafts offer the consumer relief from the plastic, prepackaged, impersonal look of manufactured products. Some of the crafts sold include leather belts and sandals, jewelry, ceramics and pottery, blown glass, macrame, batiked and handmade clothing, framed pressed flowers, pipes and other "head" items, paintings, photographs and sculptures.

Joan Fallers used to be a secretary. In March 1973, she decided that she had taken enough dictation to last a lifetime. The only "skill" she had was macrame, an occasional hobby. Since plants were becoming more popular, she started making macrame plant hangers. She sold them from a small folding table in Union Square, in the heart of San Francisco's tourist belt. "By the first day, I had only made ten of them. By one-thirty, the end of office lunch hour, I was sold out. My expenses came to about twenty dollars. I cleared forty-five dollars the first day. Since then I have become really proficient at making hangers and I also sell macrame chokers."

In Berkeley, street artists line Telegraph Avenue almost all year. But the business is seasonal. They do best during the Christmas rush. Summer and September are also good times for street artists, who sell to tourists and returning students then. The city licenses each one.

Other craftspeople follow the crafts-show circuit. They rent exhibition space in privately sponsored shows held in parking lots, fairgrounds, shopping centers, auditoriums and halls. Whatever their sales methods, they set their own schedules and pace, selling only as often as they want. The only limiting factors are demand and the number of items they can make.

Crafts can be a tricky business. The public's tastes can be very fickle. Something that sells in one area will bomb somewhere else. Fads come and go and when something becomes popular, more craftspeople make it, increasing competition. In San Francisco, street artists and their wares were so popular that the Downtown Merchants Association, run by the big department stores, pressured the Board of Supervisors (equivalent to a city council) to severely restrict areas where the artists could sell. In New York City, street artists are virtually outlawed through restrictions; they set up portable stands which can be moved quickly. Street artists easily undersell stores since they pay no rent and offer goods they make themselves, eliminating several layers of middlepeople.

Since craft supplies and tools are usually not too expensive, it doesn't take much of an investment to get started. And if nobody buys your goods, you can always give them as presents.

Most craftspeople enjoy the creative process involved in making things. "It's really satisfying to know that I made this candle which somebody is going to use. It's a very tangible thing. I have made so many candles today."

"I like to see people's reaction to my pipes. When they go

WOW and like them, it makes me feel so good. It's also a great way to meet people."

Some craftspeople use the street as a starting point, eventually running a small crafts shop, selling to retailers. They go to trade shows, hire representatives on a commission basis, or sell to nearby stores.

I know a man who started selling "liquid silver" necklaces in Berkeley during the 1972 Christmas season. By 1973 he was supplying department stores all over the country. When he got his first few wholesale orders, he had his brother sell on the street. He hired his cousin to string beads. Later his cousin supervised the shop. He sold to stores and coordinated the business. He sold Puka shells to the stores in 1974. He works about six months a year, getting suppliers and selling jewelry.

"I find it interesting. I take lots of breaks. I realize that this is part of the cycle and deal with it on the terms that I choose. I won't deal with con-men or 'hot-shots.' When stores see that you are real, that you deliver what you promise, they are happy to deal with you.

"It's actually easier than the street—although my brother still sells there. I know who my customers are, and I only have to see a few of them each day for about two months. I go to the Boutique Shows in New York and Los Angeles—I sell a lot there."

OTHER IDEAS:

Sell at flea markets.

Rent your workshop space and tools to amateur craftspeople.

Produce kits for customers to make their own crafts. One company, Jubilee Products, used to make candles; now they produce candle-making kits.

Rent an open lot or a floor of a building and open a one-day, one-month, or year-long crafts fair, subletting booth space to craftspeople.

TO FIND OUT MORE:

There are thousands of books in every store and library on how to make and produce crafts.

The American Crafts Council (44 W. 53 St., New York, NY 10019) is a national, nonprofit membership organization founded in 1943 to stimulate interest in contemporary crafts. It maintains the Museum of Contemporary Crafts in New York City, and publishes the bimonthly *Craft Horizons*. It also runs a nationwide slide/film service, a library, and an information service. It has a full line of books (catalog free).

The Craftsman's Survival Manual: Making a Full- or Part-Time Living from Your Craft (by George and Nancy Wettlaufer, Prentice-Hall, 1974) is a very fine guide which is a must for the craftsperson who is even considering relying upon his or her craft for a living. It covers getting set up in business, record-keeping, taxes, pricing, selling at shows, selling through shops, advertising, promotion and survival.

Selling Your Crafts (by Norbert N. Nelson, Van Nostrand Reinhold Co., 1967) has some very useful things to say about the business end of crafts. Plenty of food for thought—if you want your craft to feed your stomach.

The Goodfellow Catalog of Wonderful Things (by Christopher Weills, Box 4520, Berkeley, CA 94704, 1974) is a picture-book catalog of beautiful handmade crafts. If you want ideas, start here.

The Goodfellow Review of Crafts (2839 Forest Ave., Berkeley, CA 94705) is great. It covers crafts from pottery to weaving, quilting, woodworking, glass blowing, leather, iron, etc., providing designs, features on craftspeople, tips and techniques, book and resource reviews, and lists of exhibits, folk art shows, workshops, classes and crafts fairs.

The Crafts Report: The Newsmonthly of Marketing, Management and Money for Crafts Professionals (801 Wilmington Trust Bldg., Wilmington, DE 19801) lists shops and galleries, shows and fairs looking for crafts and covers conferences and guilds. How-to's (on selling, for example) are authoritatively written by craftspeople themselves.

The Crafts Fair Guide (P.O. Box 262, Mill Valley, CA 94941) is an artist-rated guide to the fairs, most of them in California. It could be useful if you live in the West and are ready to sell at fairs.

The Working Craftsman (Box 42, Northbrook, IL 60062) lists crafts fairs nationally and features articles about craftspeople and crafts.

77
DOOR-TO-DOOR SALESPERSON

Selling from door to door is an ideal job for those who enjoy selling services and products to the public on a one-to-one basis.

A young man in Des Moines, Iowa, recently sold enough encyclopedias door-to-door in one year to put himself through college.

A young woman in Villa Park, Illinois, sold Avon products during her senior year in high school; she earned spending money for her first college year while selling products she enjoys using herself.

Everywhere, tapes and records are sold door-to-door.

Fuller Brush and Watkins salespeople were for years the delight of rural housewives. They still are. A mild-mannered Fuller Brushman in Berkeley, California, in 1977 made $5 to

$10 per hour; he said territories were always open and that his customers looked forward to the Fuller Brush visits.

Many products and services can be sold door-to-door these days. But call the town or city clerk before entering a new community; some cities and towns have "Green River Ordinances," which prohibit door-to-door sales.

Develop a regular route which is serviced as infrequently as four times a year or as often as daily—depending on you and your product.

TO FIND OUT MORE:

The Direct Selling Association (1730 M St., N.W., Washington, DC 20036) publishes regular up-to-date free lists of its nearly 100 member companies and the products they sell through door-to-door salespeople.

═══78═══
SCREEN MOVIES

There is a lot of money to be made showing movies. On the most casual level, you could rent an eight- or sixteen-millimeter film projector and present sports or stag films or esoteric movies.

At another level, you could rent a building or loft and convert it into a small theater. Such a theater opened several years ago in Monte Rio, California, in what used to be a factory. You've got to be aware of the tastes of your customers or the movie will play to an empty house. In Monte Rio, the theater attracts mainly young alternative-culture people and teenagers. Recent films included a repeat of *Monterey Pop*, several Woody Allen films, and a repeat of *One Flew Over the Cuckoo's Nest*.

But there are other ways to make money on movies. For instance, an Elmhurst, Illinois, leftist group found that owning a print of an unusual and unique movie—the Chicago '68 Yippie film—could draw an audience for a benefit. They reserved a Sunday afternoon at a local church coffeehouse, charged admission, and played their film as well as several others they borrowed from peace, social justice and women's groups in Chicago. The coffeehouse charged them nothing, but made money selling soda pop, coffee and snacks.

A Sante Fe man had another idea. He discovered how cheap it was to rent right-wing films from the John Birch Society, the Nazis, and others. He rented church halls and advertised the showings in underground newspapers. He made money.

An Austin group put together a "Women's Film Festival" on consecutive Sunday afternoons. They persuaded a movie house to join their efforts. The place was filled to overflowing, during a time when the theater was usually half-empty.

OTHER IDEAS:

Put together film festivals for holidays like Halloween, Thanksgiving and Memorial Day.

TO FIND OUT MORE:

Motion Picture Market Place (ed. by Tom Costner, Little, Brown & Co., 1976; annual) lists distributors of films—shorts, features, documentaries and X-rated films—as well as sources for projection equipment and a great number of resources for the filmmaker.

The Film-Makers' Cooperative (175 Lexington Ave., New York, NY 10016) is an ideal source for independent films. Films are listed and rented on the filmmakers' own terms and in their behalf. The catalog of films is free (they ask for donations and don't demand them). They'll also tell you about other distributors of independent films, "believing that the audience for film far outnumbers existing or potential sources."

The National Association of Theater Owners (1500 Broadway, New York, NY 10036) may be helpful.

Educational Film Library Association (43 W. 61 St., New York, NY 10023; information free) publishes filmographies (annotated listings of films) on aging, alternatives, American issues, etc. It has also recently published the *16mm Distribution Handbook,* with a chapter on commercial theaters that screen independent films. When you're set up, you may want to be listed. And contacting fellow theater-owners as you travel would be valuable.

Among those who rent movies and films is Films Incorporated, 1144 Wilmette Ave., Wilmette, IL 60091, with over 5000 titles. Western World Productions, P.O. Box 3594, San Francisco, CA 94119, rents independent, low-budget productions.

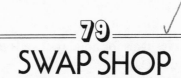

79
SWAP SHOP

Running a swap shop is as good as running a used-book store— you get first pick of the merchandise and you make money selling the rest.

Basically, you buy used furniture, lamps, books, knickknacks, and other household items for roughly one-third to one-half of what you think you can sell them for. Or you trade on the same value basis, taking two and giving one if the three items are the same value.

In Riverton, Wyoming, a woman runs a swap shop out of her double garage. Her best day is Saturday, when furniture is constantly moving in and out. She advertises in the garage-sale classifieds in the local newspaper. And she has signs posted in various spots around her neighborhood advertising her alley location.

In many ways, running a swap shop is like running a permanent garage sale. Consider taking other people's furniture and selling it for a commission if you can't buy it outright. Consider combining this with junk collecting. Check with your local police department; they may have rules or suggestions to avoid taking in stolen merchandise.

═ 80 ═
PARTY SALESPERSON

Parties are a great way to sell merchandise. In fact, parties have made Tupperware a household word. Political candidates have been sold to voters at parties and "coffees" for years. Now, the number of consumer products being sold at parties is growing immensely. The party idea is a selling technique that really works.

Besides Tupperware, products currently being marketed through parties include cosmetics, copperware, pots and pans, and toys. Toy parties held six to ten weeks before Christmas are usually very successful.

What else can be sold at parties? Auto repair equipment sells well when it is offered at a "repair training party." Sell tune-up equipment (timing strobe lights, spark plugs, spark plug wrenches, points, etc.) and demonstrate how repairs are done. Give free booklets of step-by-step instructions. You can sell safety kits (spot lights, flashing red lights, hand wrenches, candles, first-aid kits, fuses, SCS flags, etc.); oil, oil filters and oil filter wrenches; winter tank heaters, and other items. With the outrageous cost of auto repairs, everybody is doing their own tune-ups, repairs and oil changes.

Drug paraphernalia is sometimes sold at parties—and there are plenty of items to choose from. For instance, there are thousands of pipe styles: antler and phallic pipes, bongs, water-pipes, and even pens which convert to hash pipes. Other items include marijuana-leaf keychains, marijuana growers' books, Ozium aerosol smell-killer, coke kits, roach clips, stashes, men-tholated rolling papers, grass cleaners, T-shirts, cleaning bowls, scales, and drug jewelry, such as silver replicas of Quaaludes.

You can also sell gift items and stationery, candles, ashtrays, glasses, or outdoor and wilderness equipment at parties.

First decide what kind of products you want to sell. Study the products on the market and pick particular products that you think will sell well. By perusing various stores in large metropolitan areas, you should come up with a number of products you can sell, as well as the names of their manufacturers. Wholesale catalogs offer an even more varied selection.

Contact the manufacturers, or check the Yellow Pages of your nearest large city for suppliers and distributors. Trade journals can supply you with names and addresses of manufac-turers and suppliers in their field—and many public libraries have lists of nearly every trade journal in every field in the country. You could also check the *Thomas Register,* found in large libraries, for the manufacturer of a specific product.

Contact the manufacturer or supplier. Tell them your plans —that you'd like to sell their products at parties—and ask for their help. They could give it gladly, since it means more sales for them. You'll need samples or a catalog with a description and illustration of each item. Suppliers may give you samples. Or you may have to buy them, in which case you should try to make arrangements for incentives. One deal might be that you get the tenth item free when you buy nine at wholesale.

Then invite all your friends and acquaintances to your party. Send written or printed invitations. Have refreshments. And, of course, have your display items out for all to see. Demonstrate their use, point out the advantages of owning such items, sell, sell, sell. Take orders. And when the items are shipped to you by your supplier, deliver.

If nothing else, it's one hell of an excuse to hold a party.

Once you've mastered party sales, franchise by having other people hold parties. This is how Tupperware sells so much. Party hosts and hostesses are given free products and a small percentage of the evening's receipts for providing coffee and snacks, their living rooms, and their friends and acquaintances to whom you give your pitch.

OTHER IDEAS:

Sell personalized goods at parties.

Hold plant parties, offering hosts/hostesses free plants. Offering growing hints (in a class- or seminar-oriented party) will draw interest and encourage guests to buy.

TO FIND OUT MORE:

The Direct Selling Association (1730 M St., N.W., Washington, DC 20036) publishes regular up-to-date free lists of its nearly 100 member companies and the products they sell through party plans. (But don't let your imagination be limited to these companies.)

=81=
LAUNDROMAT OWNER

Laundromats are used primarily by apartment dwellers, the young, and the poor. They provide a basic service for people who do not own their own washers; such people patronize Laundromats no matter what the state of the economy.

The ideal location for a Laundromat is a storefront, but even a large garage with plenty of water and drainage near apartments or where young and poor people live might work.

One family in Riverton, Wyoming, runs both a motel and the attached Laundromat next door. They have a Dutch door between the Laundromat and their living room, which serves as a counter for change or complaints about the machines. Both businesses require someone to be on duty most of the day, yet neither business requires constant attention.

OTHER IDEAS:

Run a laundry and ironing service in your Laundromat.

Install automatic dry-cleaning machines; they are used by many economy-minded people.

82
VENDING MACHINE
ROUTE OWNER

Vending machines are available for lease or for sale. They can vend virtually anything, so keep nontraditional uses in mind. For example, cigarette rolling papers may be vended. In northern California during the 1977 drought, water that tasted good was sold in vending machines (10¢ per half gallon, provide your own container, for tap water that's been treated and purified). In many states, prophylactics are sold from restroom vending machines in gas stations and restaurants. In many apartment buildings, there are milk and cigarette machines. Along the interstate highways, rest areas are equipped with vending machines which sell everything from playing cards to toothbrush/ toothpaste sets in bathrooms and food machines which vend everything from soup to nuts.

Many landlords and business people are happy to have you set up the vending machines and pay them small rents or percentages. Gas stations and restrooms are common locations. Businesses may jump at the chance to offer their employees vended snacks and drinks. Fraternity houses, dormitories, and apartment-building lobbies are often choice locations for machines.

You'll need to purchase machines. sell locations, install your machines, stock them regularly, service and repair them, and deal with collecting and counting coins.

OTHER IDEAS:

Be an independent newspaper vendor. Establish a route by buying used newsracks and selling a popular paper/magazine not readily available. In many cities, no license is required.

Buy old vending machines and repair/refurbish them for resale or to start your own route. Mechanical non-electric machines' resale value has declined as the new electronic machines gain wider acceptance. But owners of some establishments prefer the older ones because they are easily repaired. Some institutions use machines to apportion food such as fruit, milk, yogurt, nuts and other wholesome goodies. In these cases, the coin requirements are usually eliminated.

TO FIND OUT MORE:

Blue Book of Automatic Merchandising (published periodically; National Automatic Merchandising Association, 7 South Dearborn St., Chicago, IL 60603) lists manufacturers of machines, vendable products suppliers, etc.

The National Automatic Merchandising Association (7 S. Dearborn St., Chicago, IL 60603) is the trade organization representing the vending industry. It offers information and assistance. And its director of public relations, Walter W. Reed, wrote the Small Business Administration's excellent 70-page book, "Starting and Managing a Small Automatic Vending Business." Buy this one first.

You can probably purchase vending machines most cheaply by looking for used machines right in your own community or area. New and reconditioned machines are available from many sources, including Parkway Machine Corp., 1930 Greenspring Dr., Timonium, MD 21093. This company, and many others, will send a catalog on request.

83
RENT MACHINE TIME

Americans love machines, labor-saving devices and expensive toys. But they are sometimes just too expensive to buy for occasional use, which is the *raison d'être* for rental agencies.

Rent video portapacks, minicomputers, minicomputer time, car racks, tools, pinball machines, cameras, projectors, studio space, roto-tillers, or any other "machine" that people use infrequently.

Or just rent tools. A New England gardener, for example, bought a roto-tiller for $500 and rents it out for $16 a day.

In Sacramento, Jack Trend rents videorecording outfits complete with camera crew for $175 to videotape you reading your own will for showing after your death.

In Raleigh, North Carolina, Bob Munnerlyn opened Bob's Rent-a-Wreck, Inc., offering rental car customers banged-up bargains.

Two rental fields which are not saturated are motorcycle rentals and bicycle/motorbike leasing.

TO FIND OUT MORE:

Rental Equipment Register (free to qualified rental dealers and equipment dealers; 2048 Cotner Ave., Los Angeles, CA 90025) is a business magazine devoted to the equipment rental industry, including firms that rent tools, trucks, trailers, camping/recreation equipment, construction equipment, sickroom and party supplies. It has many articles on successful operations. Valuable. *Rental Equipment Rate Guide,* by the same publishers, lists suggested minimums, daily, weekly and monthly rental rates, and also gives information on billing procedures and delivery and overtime charges.

The American Rental Association (2920 23 Ave., Moline, IL 61265) is a professional trade association for the equipment rental industry. Members receive the monthly *Rental Age* magazine, are listed in the membership directory, receive legislative and administrative manuals and materials, and get advertising help and promotional materials.

84
RUN A PHYSICAL/EMOTIONAL CONDITIONING CENTER

How much would you pay to spend an hour in a sauna, Lilly isolation tank, hot tub, whirlpool or steam room? To spend a half hour hooked up to biofeedback machines to learn how to drop into alpha? To listen to a relaxation/hypnosis tape after a stressful day?

The Samadhi Isolation Tank (2123 Lakeshore Ave., Los Angeles, CA 90039) sells for about $2000. Several San Francisco owners are selling time in their tanks at $10 or $15 per hour.

Synergy, a northern California organization, sells computerized over-the-phone stress relief for $15. You send in your money. They send you a questionnaire. You call the computer and read in your answers to the questions. The computer charts the anxiety levels in your voice, then mails you a ten-day program for reducing stress in your life.

An Ohio woman has invested a great deal of money in a trampoline, weights, and other body-building equipment. But she uses them only for an hour or so a day. So she rents out time in her home gym—primarily to other women. She works with her neighbors, friends, and other customers in developing programs for stamina, strength and slimming down.

OTHER IDEAS:

Run a trip center for people who are high on drugs of various types. It should be comfortable, relaxing, and filled with amusements a psychedelicized individual might enjoy.

85
MAIL ORDER

Magazines constantly carry advertisements titled "How You Can Make a Fortune in Mail Order" and "Gross $100,000 the First Year." These claims may be exaggerations, but mail order is definitely a lucrative, low-effort business. For proof, look at all the mail-order ads on TV, radio, magazines, newspapers, matchbooks and food packages, and offers through the mail and in restaurants, stores and public places (usually with tear-off coupons). Companies would not advertise unless they were making money.

The chances are good that you bought this book from a mail-order company. It selected various magazines whose readers would probably be interested in this subject. Possibly you were reading a magazine, saw this ad, and sent in your money.

The first rule of any business is know your market. In mail order, you want to reach the largest number of people who might become interested in your products, at the lowest cost per person. Obviously, you wouldn't sell fishing lures in a magazine for brides. There are thousands of magazines, each with a slightly different readership. Choose the ones with a readership which matches your product.

Or you might decide to buy a spot on a local radio or TV station. Where to advertise is an important decision—it could mean your venture's success or failure.

Choosing a product can be a difficult decision. It is easier if you have a working knowledge of the field. You must know which people are in it, what they want, and how to present your product to them.

Perhaps you are making a craft item; mail order may be the way to sell it. Usually, though, mail-order companies buy the products they sell from a manufacturer or distributor. They pay one-third of retail or two-thirds of wholesale. With handling, packaging and shipping, the total cost of the product and handling should come to no more than 50 percent of the price you sell it for. Advertising costs should add another 10 to 40 percent, leaving you a profit of between 10 and 40 percent.

Let's say that you have chosen a particular product and decided where to advertise it. Design the advertisement or get it designed for you, place it, and wait for orders to roll in. Deposit the checks, ship the orders, and place another ad.

Mail order can be a tricky business. You must be sure of your source of supply: Mail-order companies have gone under because they couldn't fill orders they had received and were forced to return their customers' money. There are other hazards:

bad checks, poorly selling products, and defective merchandise.

With a little foresight and carefully selected merchandise, the chances are good that you can make a living in mail order.

OTHER IDEAS:

Deal in mailing lists: Sell or trade the customer list you've accumulated to other mail-order firms.

Sell per-piece insertions in your mailings to other companies.

Use bounce-backs: Drop new ads for different products into the package in which you ship each order.

TO FIND OUT MORE:

How to Win Success in the Mail-Order Business (Arco, 1972): Reading this book will make you glad you did. It suggests caution, yet is optimistic. And it's filled with tips, information and know-how—on starting a mail-order business and on running it profitably.

How to Start and Run a Successful Mail-Order Business (by Sean Martyn, David McKay Co., 1974) is detailed and informative, from products to selling to ad-writing. Good, solid advice.

The Mailing List Brokers Professional Association (541 Lexington Ave., New York, NY 10022) is a membership association for customer list brokers. Membership by the broker from whom you're buying your mailing lists may offer you some degree of confidence in that firm's reliability.

The Small Business Administration (Supt. of Documents, U.S. Government Printing Office, Washington, DC 20402) offers three useful publications: *Mail Order Retailing by Small Enterprises, Selling by Mail Order* and *National Mailing List Houses.*

86
FUNDRAISER/
WRITE A GRANT

Organizational fundraisers work for mentally and physically handicapped groups, disadvantaged children, volunteer bureaus, VD clinics, political groups, summer camps, health problem agencies, churches and church agencies, public interest groups, universities, the arts, even their own projects (see Low-Budget Movie Producer).

Fundraisers may run Bike-A-Thons, variety shows, telephone solicitation campaigns, white elephant sales, flea markets, bazaars, garage sales, or Walk-A-Thons. Some fundraisers visit or solicit rich patrons or alumni.

In San Francisco, a fundraising dinner for night-lighting the Palace of Fine Arts included a lavish hotel banquet complete with wines donated by a historic winery, speakers, and a film, as well as a display of rare photos and memorabilia, all for $27.50 per person.

Fundraisers often call upon stars in many fields to help raise money. Donny and Marie Osmond helped kicked off the March of Dimes Super-Walk in the Bay area one year. Two years earlier, the Allman Brothers gave benefit concerts for then-almost-unknown Jimmy Carter's campaign fund.

Many fundraisers use volunteers and make considerable efforts in recruiting them.

Fundraisers sometimes write grant proposals. They may contract their services for a fee or take a percentage of the funds they raise.

TO FIND OUT MORE:

The Bread Game (Glide Publications, 330 Ellis, San Francisco, CA 94102, 1974) is one of the best books around on how to go after a grant. It offers a step-by-step guide.

While You're Up, Get Me a Grant: A Basic Bibliography (by Nancy Elnor, Elizabeth Katz, Martha Powers, Bay Area SRRT, 2745 Stuart #3, Berkeley, CA 94705) is a ten-page bibliography by librarians to provide a starting point for foundation fundraising. It could be very helpful.

The Nonprofit Money Game (Junior League of Washington, 3039 M Street, N.W., Washington, DC 20007, 1975) is a 32-page outline of fundraising possibilities —as valuable as a book twice its size.

America's Most Successful Fund Raising Letters (ed. by Joseph Dermer, Public Service Materials Center, 355 Lexington Ave., New York, NY 10017, 1976) is a compilation of the most successful fundraising letters used by colleges and universities, hospitals, social welfare agencies, private schools, churches, etc. Very valuable.

Creative Book Company (P.O. Box 214998, Sacramento, CA 95821) publishes several books of use to fundraisers. They include *How to Write a Winning Proposal, Treasure in Your Trash* (on organizational junk and rummage sales), *Walking for Fun and Funds* and *How to Produce Effective Slide Tape Talks*.

The Proposal Writer's Swipe File II: 14 Professionally Written Grant Proposals: Prototypes of Approaches, Styles and Structures (ed. by Jean Brodsky, Taft Products, Inc., 1000 Vermont Ave., N.W., Washington, DC 20005, 1976) is a representation of successful grant proposals from a variety of nonprofit sectors —education, religion, the arts, communications, conservation, etc. Very valuable.

87
TAPE-RECORDING EVENTS/ LECTURES AND SELLING

A Santa Barbara businessman invited his 16-year-old son along to a business conference. He thought the boy would benefit from the meeting. Indeed he did. It was the start of a rapidly growing business which the young man now runs full time.

The boy tape-recorded each of the lectures at the conference. Interested conferees asked for copies of the tapes; some had missed speeches that they later heard were excellent, and others wanted to hear particular speeches a second or third time.

Now he records many conferences, lectures and other audio events in his area. He sets up tables at many events to sell his tapes directly to conferees. He also advertises his tapes in organizational magazines immediately following the events.

OTHER IDEAS:

Make tape-recordings of spiritual gatherings for sale to believers.

Tape-record class lectures for sale to students.

88
INTERSTATE/
INTERNATIONAL SELLER

Traders travel from country to country and from one part of the U.S. to another, buying, selling and trading. These people are not smuggling—their trading is legal.

Market differences between locales determine the products you can trade. The automobile van market in New York, for example, offers lower prices than does the same market in California. One trader purchases vans in New York and drives them to California, where he sells them for a profit, and drives (in a drive-away car) back to New York with a load of antique clothing and old Hawaiian shirts.

The market differences between city and country are sometimes phenomenal. Cameras and jewelry are priced hundreds of dollars higher in rural areas than in New York and other metropolitan areas. An Ohio student financed his college education making runs to New York for record albums.

The market conditions between the mainland (the 48 contiguous states) and Alaska and Hawaii also differ tremendously.

PART VI
MOTOR SKILLS

89
MAKE/REPAIR
MUSICAL INSTRUMENTS

A young woman in Martha's Vineyard sells handmade bamboo flutes for a living. She made them when she was in Jamaica.

My uncle took a course in piano tuning when he retired from his job early. It became a lucrative second career.

In Brooklyn, New York, an immigrant from Appalachia makes dulcimers by hand.

Handmade guitars and custom-made instruments in general are experiencing a revival. And wherever there are instruments, whether made in a factory or at home, there is need for instrument repairs.

TO FIND OUT MORE:

Piano Tuning: A Simple and Accurate Method for Amateurs (by J. Cree Fischer, Dover, 1975) starts from the beginning with piano theory and construction. Then it suggests remedies and repairs (for loose keys, for example). Finally, it devotes a hundred pages to tuning by ear.

Professional Piano Tuning (by W. Dean Howell, American Piano Supply Co., Box 1055, Clifton, NJ, 1969) says you will take up to eight hours tuning your first piano, while the seasoned professional takes less than two hours. It will guide you through the process, from tools to technique.

90

AUTO/
MOTORCYCLE REPAIRS

Every car requires periodic maintenance, but a tremendous number of Americans don't trust the people who fix their cars and often feel they are overcharged.

If you are skilled at fixing cars or motorcycles, don't mind getting greasy, and enjoy the labor, this is an ideal way for you to earn money. Even if you just change oil at cheaper rates than the service station down the street, you'll attract more than enough business.

One fellow in Berkeley rents a back yard and driveway. In the driveway, he's installed a frame for a block and tackle; he uses it whenever he has to pull an engine. He's willing to do almost any engine, transmission or clutch work imaginable. In the back yard, he works on engines and other parts he has removed. He has a fully equipped workbench there.

One company offers "a complete expert tune-up by an unemployed class A mechanic." The four-by-four-inch flyer (they're distributed under windshield wipers) gives a phone number, declines payment by check, and lists prices for four-, six- and eight-cylinder cars.

OTHER IDEAS:

Add a ramp to your truck or van and advertise as a motorcycle towing service—in most places, regular towing services don't handle bikes.

TO FIND OUT MORE:

Automotive Marketing Directory (Irving-Cloud Publishing Co., 7300 N. Cicero Ave., Chicago, IL 60646) lists parts rebuilders, automotive jobbers and distributors, trade associations, and manufacturers.

Chilton Book Company, Radnor, Pennsylvania, is well known for its authoritative auto and motorcycle service manuals. Many of them are probably at the reference desk in your library.

Automotive Service Business: Operation and Management (by William H. Crouse, McGraw-Hill, 1973) covers the business from one end to the other. It's a must.

Fixing Cars: A People's Primer (by Rick Greenspan et al., San Francisco Institute of Automotive Ecology, 1974) offers advice for beginners and explains the principles of auto mechanics by comparing the car with the human body. If you need this book, you're not ready to charge for your services, but you may be able to avoid paying someone else.

91
REMAIL/TELEPHONE ANSWERING SERVICE

Jerry and Peter were partners in a small moving business for six years. They were making a good living but were getting tired of the labor.

"We thought about a grocery store, but you have to lug those boxes—which are heavy. The hours are no bargain either.

We used an answering service for our moving business . . . if San Francisco could use another grocery store, it could use another post office box rental and answering service."

Answering services are growing in popularity. People who are "out of town on business" or away often use them. Other people use them to screen out undesirable callers or in place of a home phone.

People rent private mailboxes when there are no post office box vacancies; when they do not want to deal directly with the postal service; when they want to start a business but have no office and don't want to receive mail at home; when they need mail forwarded because they're out of town on business often; when they want to postmark mail from a city other than their own; or when they simply want to remain anonymous.

Jerry and Peter opened their service by renting an office in downtown San Francisco. Jerry was licensed by the postal service to act as an agent after a brief investigation. He advertises "in every local paper and magazine I can get my hands on." These include two entertainment magazines, the local alternative and underground papers, ten suburban weeklies, and five gay or sex papers. "We put up tear-off pads in Laundromats all over the city and suburbs. We cover over three hundred of them. I figure over a million people see our ads."

After five months, Post Rent-A-Box broke even. Three hundred people use Post's number as their own and call in for messages. Five hundred people use their box rental services.

Post keeps the office open from 8:30 to 6:30. "It will eventually be a twenty-four-hour-a-day service." It has three telephone lines, which are always ringing. The post office boxes are folders in a file cabinet.

A remail service is an answer to many problems. It can work in two ways: A remail service can be your mailing address when you're on the move (much like having a private post office box which forwards your mail), or you can use it to forward letters as though they were first mailed from another city.

What's this "forwarding letters" all about? It works like this:

The remail service places classified ads in a number of national magazines—they might read, "Remails, 50¢, Black, Box 212, Cleveland, Ohio." Then someone who lives somewhere other than Cleveland—someone who wants to send a letter but doesn't want to be located—sends the addressed, stamped envelope to "Black" in Cleveland along with 50¢. Black mails the letter from Cleveland and pockets the 50¢.

You need a mailing address or post office box to run a mail-forwarding service. Place ads—preferably in magazines which already carry such ads. And "key" your ads—if you advertise in *Popular Automobiles*, for example, add "Dept. PA" to your address. The "key" allows you to judge the effectiveness of each ad you've placed.

A remail service can also offer the person who moves often a permanent mailing address. In this case, the person pays a monthly fee; the remail service holds the client's mail until it is picked up. Or the remail service, for an extra fee, will forward the mail to another address. *TAP*, the phone phreak's newsletter, uses such a service to avoid letting the postal service know who's publishing the newsletter. Joe White, on the other hand, uses such a service because he travels quite a lot and has more confidence that a private forwarding service will get his mail to him than that the postal service will.

Whatever the reasons people use it, you can make money running a remail service. Running ads in national magazines can teach you the principles of the mail-order business—and since you've already rented a post office box, you might as well run two businesses through it as one. If you've rented an office where people can pick up their mail, you could just as well put in a telephone line or two and run a telephone answering service and a wake-up service.

OTHER IDEAS:

Start a WATS (Wide Area Telephone Service; 800- numbers) line service. WATS line customers pay the phone company a flat rate, then can receive or make unlimited long-distance phone calls. WATS line services accept telephone orders and messages from various companies' customers, and bill the companies for each call.

<h1>═══92═══
WOODWORKER/
FURNITURE/CABINET MAKER</h1>

Making furniture and building cabinets offer woodworkers fun and profit. Almost anyone can learn woodworking, and it can provide income and earnings from the earliest stages of proficiency.

There are many books and magazines which lay out plans for various types of furniture and cabinets. Many lumber yards carry simple furniture kits of raw lumber and accessories for you to construct and assemble. Or design your own.

You'll need to build samples to show folks who are interested. They may buy what you've already constructed. But some people want something entirely different and may want you to create it.

OTHER IDEAS:

Specialize in furniture which "knocks down" for moving.

Specialize in unfinished fine furniture, for the growing number of Americans who want to finish their own furniture. In Salinas, California, five friends started Heartwood Kit Furniture, which provides solid wood components, clear instructions, hardware, and all the finishing supplies and tools, plus cushions with your choice of fabrics. The furniture is simple and fairly inexpensive, yet is comfortable and looks good.

Combine this with junk collecting: Create new designs in furniture from wood others have thrown away (wooden crates into couches, for example); it's an art form. This End Up, a North Carolina company, was started by two broke friends who dragged an Early Shipping Crate couch to a flea market and started taking orders.

Specialize in constructing outdoor woodwork such as picnic tables and benches, picket fences, trellises, sandboxes and playhouses.

A number of people sell sections of tree trunks for tables and tabletops.

Specialize in constructing children's furniture or in making antique-looking furniture.

93
TV/RADIO/ ELECTRONICS REPAIRS

Fixing radios, televisions, stereos and tape recorders requires skill, which develops quickly and naturally for those who are excited by the electronics field; the many who have built radios and other electronic equipment from scratch or kits and who read the electronics magazines avidly are well on their way to being capable of performing radio and television repairs.

One Iowa man started his radio/television repair business when he was 14. He had built a number of projects from kits and from scratch and had become an amateur (ham) radio operator. He decided to make it pay; he bought a city business license and repaired sets for his family and friends.

TO FIND OUT MORE:

101 TV Troubles: From Symptom to Repair (by Art Margolis, Tab Books, Blue Ridge Summit, PA 17214, 1969) will get you through many TV repair problems. This and some electronic knowledge will get you far.

Photofact Service (from Howard W. Sams & Co., Indianapolis, IN) may even be found in your library! There's a packet of information, complete with pictorial and schematic diagrams and service notes, for every U.S. television and radio model—and a good many foreign ones, too.

94
LOCKSMITH

Locksmiths are in demand. We move into new homes and change all the door lock tumblers. We lock ourselves out of our cars. We need extra keys made. We need advice on better protection for our homes and offices.

Locksmiths provide it all. Learn the skills, buy the tools, get the licenses, and you're in business.

OTHER IDEAS:

Set up your mobile key-duplicating service at flea markets and fairs.

TO FIND OUT MORE:

The Locksmithing Institute (a division of Technical Home Study Schools, 1500 Cardinal Dr., Little Falls, NJ 07424) offers a home-study course and claims to be the oldest and largest locksmithing school in the world. It publishes a newsletter for its graduates.

══════ 95 ══════
SEWING AND DECORATION

Clothesmaking, sewing and decoration are some of the most underrated skills in this country. We have often asked people about their skills and they never even consider sewing as a possible source of income. With just a sewing machine, an embroidery needle or some dye, you can start your own business. There are many more possibilities than can be discussed here.

Custom-made shirts, slacks and dresses are always in demand. Since you are selling directly to your customer, eliminating three or four middlepeople, you can sell at prices competitive with ready-to-wear. Clothing manufacturers frequently post signs on bulletin boards, and run ads in the local classified section.

Stores often buy handmade ready-to-wear. Some stores take garments on consignment only. Before you start sewing, talk with the store buyers. Take along some samples of your best work. And discuss items, styles and store policy.

Local professional theater companies frequently have costumes made by local people. A woman I know worked for the Shakespearean Festival in Ashland, Oregon. After two seasons' experience, she moved to Nova Scotia, where she makes costumes each spring for a local repertory company. She also makes stage costumes for local bands.

A man I know got a job tying leather suits with rawhide thongs. A year and a half later he went into partnership with a cutter. They put together only four suits a week. That takes them about three days. "Jim and I like to fish a lot, and they bite all year 'round here. We don't advertise or nothin', but somebody wears a pair of our pants and people ask him where he got them."

A woman in New York City makes dresses and new jeans from used denim and '40's-style upholstery fabric. She buys the used denim in bulk from the Salvation Army. It costs her a dollar a pound. She says she could sell 100 garments a week, but gets a chance to make only 15 to 20. "I hate weekends, so I spend them with my machine." Each Monday she delivers her newly made garments to a jeans store.

There is a man in Austin, Texas, who goes to different boutiques with his airbrush. He custom-paints shirts for their customers (at $8 an hour).

Frequently, laundries and dry cleaners will give alteration and repair work to independents. They can also refer customers to you.

There is a steady demand for fashion batik and tie-dye clothing and cloth. A small company in Berkeley dips T-shirts in wax, cracks it, then dyes the shirts, mass-producing inexpensive colorful batiks.

Other people do embroidery, decoupage, bead and sequin work, drapes and curtains, flags and banners, and bridal gowns.

One store on Greenwich Avenue in New York sells every item of clothing in its shop for $10. Most of the clothing is satin.

And all of it is sewn in the back room. They will, of course, tailor clothing to your body for $35. The clothes on the racks, from shirts to leisure suits to pants to caps, are all standard sizes with unfinished cuffs.

The success of your business will depend on repeat customers and word-of-mouth. Once you have a steady following, you will have no problem selling all you can make, but it may take a while to develop a retail trade, so be prepared to deal with an initial low-income situation.

OTHER IDEAS:

Specialize in maternity clothes, baby clothes, tablecloths, upholstery covers, placemats, cloth dolls, or toys. Or try alterations, zipper repairs, patches or decorations.

Use industrial-type machines to make or mend canvas, boat and machinery covers and sails. Make duffel bags, rugs and harnesses.

Sew nylon down jackets and outerwear.

Teach sewing and decoration.

96
PILLOW/
CUSHION/QUILT MAKER

If you enjoy sewing a great deal, making pillows, cushions and quilts may be an ideal way for you to make a living.

Quilts take hours and hours to design and sew, but sell for a lot of money—the handsewn comforter is a new status symbol. Knitted and crocheted afghans also take time to make and are expensive.

Pillows and cushions, on the other hand, can be sewn quickly by machine, and then stuffed.

One Berkeley pillowmaker offers customers their choice of dozens of styles and colors of presewn covers, which he'll fill with their choice of stuffing, from a natural tree fiber to polyester to foam. He charges from $1 for a one-foot-square pillow to $25 for his largest size.

OTHER IDEAS:

Louise Fischer sews "scene quilts" of buildings and streets in her neighborhood and sells them for $600 to $1200.

Customize pet quilts or pillows for animal lovers.

══════ 97 ══════
BREAD/CAKE/ COOKIE BAKER AND CANDY MAKER

When Nancy Pood of Sausalito's Pine Street Bakery baked the first of the six-inch-diameter chocolate chip cookies, she says people laughed at her idea and told her it would never make money. She delivered the cookies to stores—often neighborhood groceries and quick-trip shops—and displayed them in fat glass cookie jars with bell lids. They originally sold for 50¢ each and are now up to $1 and more in some stores. She's built a cookie-in-a-jar empire and now has four other bakeries competing with her for 300 outlets in the San Francisco Bay area.

The fat glass cookie jars are also being filled with smaller cookies these days. They sell for less and move quickly.

A tray of brownies, toffee and fudge sits on the counter of a truck stop along the interstate in Kansas. Each piece is wrapped in plastic. The local high-school student who makes them delivers her product to a dozen different restaurants, cafes and service stations along the interstate as well as in town.

If you bake organic breads and goodies, you'll find a ready market in health-food stores, as well as in discriminating supermarkets. Or start a bread route. Advertise that you deliver your homemade bread the day it's baked. Your customers will like the freshness of your bread as well as the personal contact with a baker that your bread route provides.

OTHER IDEAS:

Bake seasonal or holiday favorites: rum and fruit cakes, Christmas candies, handmade chocolates, or pumpkin, mince, apple, berry or fruit pies.

Bake special diet foods, such as low-salt bread.

Bake ethnic goodies, such as bagels, or Danish, French or Viennese pastry.

98

MANUFACTURER OF BIRDHOUSES, CUTTING BOARDS, TOYS AND OTHER SMALL WOODEN PRODUCTS

Good with wood? Try manufacturing small wooden products. Your product line is limited only by your imagination. Fine wooden products are always in demand.

Products include birdhouses, cutting boards (a design cut from wood with a jigsaw, for example, or a butcher block), toys (well-built toys for toddlers which are durable sell well), butcher block tabletops, fruit bowls, duck calls, duck decoys, salt and pepper shakers, chessboards, and stash boxes.

Sell your products at craft stores, craft fairs, flea markets, gift stores, head shops, department stores and specialty shops.

OTHER IDEAS:

Make and sell hand-carved signs ("Hang out a hand-carved shingle").

Carve reliefs for doors.

Sculpt small wooden pieces (small decorative sculptures sell well in gift stores).

Specialize in one product, such as stash/jewelry boxes or pipe racks.

Make woodworking kits which include the rough finished lumber, tools, and finishing goods needed to complete the project.

Turn barn boards into picture frames and art objects.

TO FIND OUT MORE:

If you're interested in toymaking for profit, be sure to write Love-Built Toys and Crafts (2907 Lake Forest Rd., P.O. Box 5459, Tahoe City, CA 95730) for their free Special Info Sheet #3, which is filled with ideas on marketing your toys. They also sell plans and parts for wooden home-built toys.

Folk Art Toys and Furniture for Children (by Joyce Davies Hundley and Jeanne Davies Muller, Doubleday, 1975) is filled with plans for such toys as a rocking horse, dollhouses, a doll cradle and a toy chest.

America in Miniatures: How to Make Models of Early American Houses, Furniture and Vehicles (by C. J. Maginley, Harcourt Brace Jovanovich, 1976) is straightforward. Model-making from wood is not the simplest art, but it's helped considerably by this guide.

Making Toys in Wood (by Charles H. Hayward, Drake, 1972) includes such projects as a miniature lawnmower, Noah's ark and animals, a doll's cot, and a wheelbarrow. The toys look as if they'd be very popular with kids and their parents.

Professor Hammerfinger's Indestructible Toys (by Steve Ross, Oliver Press, 1400 Ryan Creek Rd., Willits, CA 95490, 1975) is filled with designs which are very simple and should be easy and inexpensive to build. These are wooden toys like some which are found in nurseries these days.

Things to Make for Children (by the editors of Sunset Magazine, Lane Books, Menlo Park, CA, 1973) provides great ideas and plans for wooden toys, dollhouses, performing toys, and kids' furniture, as well as things to sew.

99

TYPIST/JUSTIFIER/ MIMEOGRAPHER

Former white collar workers tell us that it wasn't the "work" that they minded, but the office "atmosphere and politics." They felt that they were under constant stress conditions, they were sometimes supervised by petty tyrants, and they had to dress according to "dress codes." Worst of all, they had to work 40 hours a week plus traveling time during hours not of their own choosing.

Some of these people have valuable skills. Stenographers, typists and bookkeepers are all in demand as independents. They are used by small businesses, college students, writers and the general public. Notices on community and college bulletin boards and classified ads in local and city newspapers will bring results.

You will need a good electric typewriter and other office equipment. Typists usually charge by the page. Stenographers and bookkeepers charge by the hour.

You will be working at home when you want to (as long as you meet deadlines), and won't have to talk to anyone at the watercooler. You can even be totally nude when you work.

A woman I know used to work in an office typing pool. When she moved to San Francisco she leased a Compugraphic typesetting machine. It is a mini-computer about the size of a small table. As you type into it, it automatically justifies each line. Alice tells us that the machine is no harder to use than a typewriter if you are careful. She gets $10 an hour for her work.

The lease agreement comes to $6000, or $150 a month. She could have bought a guaranteed, used machine for $3500. Since she uses the machine only 24 hours a week, she sells time on it: 60 hours a week at $2 an hour, plus material (a very low price).

A Washington, D.C., typesetter uses an IBM Composer to set a number of alternative papers. His typing is so fast that he finds it more profitable to charge by the job than by the hour.

The Composer he uses is leased by one of the newspapers. He does their setting free in exchange for use of the machine for other jobs.

You could offer other business services. For instance, you could run a duplicator, stencil maker and mimeograph, or a small printer. All of these machines are easy to operate and take little training.

If you have a background in layout or graphic services, your skills are in demand. Karen used to design record and book covers for large companies. The constant pressure finally forced her to quit. Since she had many contacts in the industry, she started freelancing. Within the week she had her first job. Since she works out of her own home, with a sunny room serving as a studio, she does not have the overhead that commercial firms usually have. This gives her a definite competitive advantage. Her former assistant at her old firm is also freelancing, and they work together on big jobs.

Roger was 55 years old when he was "retired early" by the accounting firm he had worked for as a Certified Public Accountant for 30 years. He had been involved with some clients for over 15 years. As his new situation sank in, he decided to do something about it. He called his former clients and asked them to transfer their accounts. About half the companies kept him as their accountant. He opened his office, hired a recent college grad, and is making more money than ever before.

OTHER IDEAS:

Type letters, envelopes, reports, statistics, labels, postcards, etc., for nonprofits, companies or churches.

Specialize in typing term papers.

If you are familiar with computer operations, buy a mini-computer and do simple jobs for small and medium-sized organizations and companies. Projects may include accounting or bulk mail operations as well as billings.

TO FIND OUT MORE:

How to Start a Typing Service in Your Own Home (by Patricia M. Wilbanks, Arco, 1973) offers the A-to-Z of starting and running a typing service.

100
SIGN PAINTER

Painting signs is the kind of skill that can get you through a Depression: It's the kind of skill you can trade for something to eat and wear and somewhere to sleep. Woody Guthrie earned his keep at sign-painting long before his singing brought him money.

You need to be good at lettering, have an even hand, and hold an artful brush. Do a sign or two on speculation for friends. Sign your name (or your company's name) on a corner of every sign you make. List your company in the phone book, with your number or the number of your answering service.

Advertise—particularly on bulletin boards and in flea-market classified advertisers. Then sell your service store-to-store. You'll build your reputation as you go.

OTHER IDEAS:

Repaint existing signs: Pick out weathered or peeling signs in town and offer to repaint them.

Paint nameplates for homes, farms and ranches.

Paint roadside advertising signs and billboards.

=101=
CUSTOM CLOCK MAKER

Americans are very time-oriented and, as a result, buy millions of clocks each year.

The grandfather clock is one of the most sought-after, as well as most expensive, clocks in the United States. Grandfather clocks can be purchased as kits; you might build them that way, selling them for enough to pay for your labor. Or you can design your own. Once people find out you are building grandfather clocks, you'll never have a problem finding customers.

One woman recently began offering customers an inexpensive but elegant custom alarm clock. The customer brings in a photograph, which is etched onto the face of the clock—an inexpensive process. The clocks sell well and make great gifts.

A man builds custom kitchen and living-room clocks, buying the clock works from a manufacturer and building the rest out of antiqued wood, barn wood, rope, and other materials. This company customizes clocks' faces with company logo designs—a great gift for the boss or for company customers.

The cuckoo clock is also popular.

═══102═══
WELDER/ORNAMENTAL METALWORKER

Skilled welders are in demand in both urban and rural areas. Welding is a skill which many learn by following directions in a textbook; it's taught in a few weeks to high-school students and in three- or four-night sessions to 4-H Club members.

You can buy a good used electric welder and all the accessories you'll need to get started for a few hundred dollars or less. Then let your neighbors know you can repair the wheels on their lawnmowers, and let local farmers know you're for hire, as well. Price yourself competitively and offer to make house or farm calls (at least until you get established), and you'll never run out of business.

Once you're welding, if you have a creative mind, you'll be doing ornamental metalwork in no time. And you'll create demand for it by showing it to farmers and their spouses, neighbors and friends. You can weld, braze and solder mass-produced consumer items or go in for creating works of art which, of course, sell for more.

OTHER IDEAS:

One semi-retired couple packs tools in their Winnebago and finds occasional work as they travel.

There's often welding work to be found at harvest time and around boating areas.

An unemployed welder in Seattle, Washington, earns a living making welded-chain mailbox stands. Spirals sell for as much as $35.

TO FIND OUT MORE:

Welded Sculpture (by Nathan Cabot Hale, Watson-Guptill Publications, Billboard,˙ One Astor Plaza, New York, NY 10036, 1975) begins with basic welding technique, then uses it to teach welding art: shapes and figures. It covers clients, contracts, estimating costs, business aspects, and keeping yourself alive. An excellent book on the subject.

103
BICYCLE REPAIRS

Bicycles are a viable means of transportation in the United States, and are increasingly popular for recreation and fun.

Like any other machine, bicycles occasionally need repair: tires go flat, sprockets go out of line, gears need adjustment.

You can repair bicycles from your home or garage. And while you're doing it, you might seek out quality bicycle accessories to offer your customers; you might become a bicycling center, offering books, touring guides, and information; you might sell new bicycles or run a used-bicycle center.

Bulletin-board and classified advertising can bring you your first customers; word-of-mouth will keep them and their friends coming back to you.

OTHER IDEAS:

Build specialized pedal-powered vehicles, such as delivery tricycles or pedal-powered boats.

Build pedal-powered machines such as mixers, blenders, water-pumps, and grinders. They require no fuel, are low-technology items, and are healthful to run. Legs have much more power than arms and don't fatigue as easily.

Run a repair center, renting space and tool time to fix-it-yourselfers.

TO FIND OUT MORE:

Pedal-power technology is covered in many back-to-the-land magazines and manuals.

Glenn's Complete Bicycle Manual (by Clarence W. Coles and Harold T. Glenn, Crown, 1973) is big and beautiful. It covers everything and there's a photo of every step in assembling, adjusting and maintaining bikes.

104
APPLIANCE REPAIRS

It's a waste to throw out good appliances, but millions of appliances (toasters, irons, frying pans, mixers, blenders, can openers, vacuums, refrigerators, freezers, washing machines and air conditioners) are junked because of a breakdown that a simple repair could have fixed. The broken ones find their way into basements, closets and storage areas because people won't throw them away but, intimidated by electricity, won't fix them themselves either.

Small-appliance repair at best is easy and at worst still isn't so hard. If you have mechanical and electrical aptitude, you can learn how to fix appliances easily. Some manufacturers offer courses; or you can apprentice, or follow instruction books and manuals. Repair people usually specialize—in air conditioners, or small appliances, or toasters, for instance. Also consider doing simple repairs to extension cords and lamps.

Advertise. If you live in an apartment building, neighbors could be your first customers. Satisfied customers whose appliances you've repaired will spread the word. Advertise on local grocery-store bulletin boards, in advertisers and classifieds, and in the Yellow Pages.

OTHER IDEAS:

Buy non-working small appliances for a fraction of the resale price at garage sales, flea markets or secondhand stores, or from nonprofit collecting services for 25¢ to 50¢ each. Fix them and you can sell your used appliances in a store or at flea markets (make sure there's an electrical hookup so customers can try out your merchandise), or wholesale to a secondhand store.

Buy used pots and frying pans covered with grease and carbon. Clean the carbon off with household cleaning compounds and resell the kitchenware at its new higher value.

TO FIND OUT MORE:

Fix Your Small Appliances (by Jack Darr, two volumes, Howard W. Sams & Co., 1974) is a good illustrated fix-it manual for appliances as large as a vacuum cleaner. *How to Repair Major Appliances* (by Ernest Tricomi, Howard W. Sams & Co., 1971) covers the larger equipment: washers and dryers, refrigerators, etc.

How to Repair Electrical Appliances (by Gershon J. Wheeler, Reeston Publishing, Reston, VA, 1972) is a quick guide to appliance repair.

Home Appliance Servicing (by Edwin P. Anderson, Theodore Audel & Co., Howard W. Sams & Co., 1976) is a complete reference source on the subject and covers appliances large and small.

105
HAIR STYLIST/ BEAUTICIAN

Being a hair stylist or a beautician is about making people feel good and giving them pleasure. I get off on having my scalp stimulated during a shampoo, on having hot air wash my face and sweep back my hair in the drying process, and (when I'm beardless) on being lathered and shaved by a steady barber's hand.

Do well at styling hair and you'll be popular. Give pleasure as well with your cuts and you'll have more customers than you can handle.

Styling is a skill which is taught at "beauty schools" and other institutions. A degree from one of them may be required by the barber or beautician licensing laws in your state. Without a license, your business is limited to word-of-mouth. But that can be profitable, too. A San Francisco photographer gave excellent $5 hair styles to friends and their friends until his photography paid his way.

OTHER IDEAS:

Offer the pleasure alone: Give walk-in shampoos and face massages for a few bucks each.

Be a manicurist; work on people's cuticles. Be a foot beautician, preparing the skin and manicuring the toenails.

Be a makeup consultant, advising women on which cosmetics to use and the most efficient ways to use them.

Teach the art of beauty to classes. Teach classes in hair-blower use to those who still haven't got the hang of it.

Do electrolysis, removing unwanted hair permanently.

TO FIND OUT MORE:

Beauty as a Career (*by Edith Heal, Julian Messner,* 1969) is written on a junior-high level, yet has some interesting information to offer.

To become a licensed cosmetologist (which will allow you to legally perform a number of skills like manicuring, hair styling, hairdressing, etc.), you will probably be required to pass a state exam after schooling or apprenticeship. Your state cosmetology board can fill you in on details and tell you about approved schools.

Successful Salon Management for Cosmetology Students (by Edward J. Tezak, Milady Publishing, 3839 White Plains Rd., Bronx, NY 10467, 1973) covers where to locate a salon, leases, permits, financing, decorating, supplies, personnel, forms and recordkeeping, advertising and selling. This is excellent how-to information, required reading.

American Hairdresser/Salon Owner (100 Park Ave., New York, NY 10017) is the official professional publication of the National Hairdressers and Cosmetologists Association (3510 Olive St., St. Louis, MO 63103). A recent issue discussed hair and face problems, news, shows, fashion preview, salon services selling plan, how-to of skin care, hair removal, makeup, hair and hand care, the latest hair styles, and promotion and advertising.

═══ 106 ═══
FISHING LURE MAKER

If the flies you tie and the spoons you manufacture catch fish, fishermen would just as soon buy them from you as from someone else.

TO FIND OUT MORE:

Flies (by J. Edson Leonard, A.S. Barnest Co., 1960) will tell you everything—absolutely everything—you want to know about flies and how to select and tie them: over 300 pages on the subject by a man who has known, loved and studied his subject for years.

Fishing Rods: How to Make Them (by H. S. David, Dreis-Davis Co., Long Beach, CA, 1951) is a 20-page pamphlet which details the essentials of constructing your own fishing rods.

Fly-Tying: Materials, Tools, Technique (by Helen E. Shaw, Ronald Press, 1963) is a fully illustrated manual for tying flies. There is a photo for each step in the process.

107
LAMP
AND LAMPSHADE MAKER

Lamps and lampshades are simple to make and market, and there is always demand. Designer one-of-a-kind lamps sell for large sums. On the inexpensive end, "bottle lamps" made with wine bottles retail for $3 to $8.

Lamps can be made from almost any object, from an engine piston to driftwood, a flower pot, or a telephone. Lamp ideas are infinite. One coastal craftsperson makes lamps from sea-urchin shells.

OTHER IDEAS:

Make personalized lamps for children or grandparents from discarded favorite toys; make the lampshades from photos of the children.

TO FIND OUT MORE:

Making Lapshades (by Angela Fishburn, Drake, 1975) is a guide to making beautiful, distinctive handmade and hand-sewn lampshades. Complete how-to for dozens of designs.

Lampshade Making (by Phyllis M. Sharples, G. Bell & Sons, York House, Portugal St., London, WC2, 1966) is an exceptionally well-prepared guidebook to making and sewing dozens of lampshade types.

═══108═══
TYPEWRITER/
BUSINESS MACHINE SALES/
REPAIR

Jerry has built a thriving business in a tiny storefront on a residential street in Greenwich Village. He repairs, buys, sells and rents typewriters. He also sells accessories, such as ribbons. He started his repair service in the 1960's. He now has several full-time typewriter repair people. His store is crowded with typewriters, some of which were broken when he bought them for a song to repair and sell.

Typewriter repair services are always needed by businesses and students. An experienced repairperson can earn a good living.

109
TENT/KNAPSACK/
SLEEPING BAG MAKER

Quality outdoors equipment is a bargain at almost any price. Hand-sewn tents, knapsacks, sleeping bags, down coats, and other such goods offer real value. Guarantee your work and offer more value.

You could customize kits for people—Frostline (452 Burbank, Broomfield, CO 80020) sells highly recommended kits for making down clothing, pack kits, tents, bike packs, sleeping bags, comforters, and other goods. A Wyoming woman spends the fall season sewing the kits to fit her customers.

An Idaho man designs his own tents, knapsacks, and sleeping bags for Rocky Mountain wind and weather and has developed markets and customers for his products.

A California woman specializes in sewing sleeping bags and down coats customized for tall and big people. They flock to her door, since the average sleeping bag isn't long enough to keep a tall person warm.

OTHER IDEAS:

Make and repair tipis, yurts, and other portable structures. Make tarps for covering machinery and farm equipment.

=110=
SHOE AND SANDAL MAKER

A San Francisco sandal maker charges customers $35 a pair for sandals. But the customer is fitted for the sandals not once but several times during their manufacture. The finished sandals fit like a new layer of skin.

Shoe repair is a dying industry, not from lack of demand, but from lack of skilled labor. Shoe-repair people are retiring, and few young people are going into the field. Many shoe-service shops seek people to train in shoe repair.

Over 3000 pairs of fancy, expensive, hand-worked cowboy boots are turned out daily by 800 workers at a Texas plant which began years ago when the company's founder opened his own shoe-repair business and began making two or three pairs of cowboy boots a week on the side.

TO FIND OUT MORE:

Shoe Repairing (by Henry Karg, Shoe Service Institute of America, 222 W. Adams St., Chicago, IL 60606) is a basic text used in both shoe repair shops and shoe repair schools.

Starting and Managing a Small Shoe Service Shop (Superintendent of Documents, U.S. Government Printing Office, Washington, DC 20402) can help a great deal with the business aspects and details of setting up a repair business.

PART VII
MENTAL SKILLS

NEWSLETTER/
MAGAZINE PUBLISHER

Newsletter publishing is an exciting business—as a purveyor of news, you know the latest developments in your field before anyone else does. Publishing a newsletter isn't likely to make you rich—though it could—but it can provide you with a steady, growing income, month after month, year after year.

Start a newsletter about what you know. A divorced housewife in New Jersey started a newsletter made up mostly of listings of single people who were looking for dates, fun, whatever. She accepted advertising from singles bars and clubs. And she printed articles on places to go, things to do, where to meet other singles. The newsletter filled a need and was a success.

Armond Noble of Sacramento, California, quit his broadcast news job to turn his hobby into a magazine. Noble had been a ham radio operator for 24 years. He founded *Worldradio News,* which is currently sent to over 12,000 hams in dozens of countries. And, of course, Noble also converses with many of his readers over the airwaves.

What do you want to know? Would you like to know what you can get free? Start a newsletter. Perhaps call it "1200 Things You Can Get Free" and offer 100 each month. Several people in Cambridge, Massachusetts, are offering a newsletter called *Resources,* a guide to mostly free literature in a variety of special-interest areas.

199

Have you ever complained of nothing to do? Probably. Yet somewhere in your community there is probably some activity taking place right now that you don't even know about. Publish a newsletter which lists community events, activities, concerts, speeches, etc.

Publish a newsletter on activities for children, events for teenagers, or entertainment for families. Sell advertising space in the newsletter to as many of the places you mention as possible.

Newsletters are published on thousands of subjects, ranging from hobbies, entertainment listings, raising children, fashion, and geographical regions to finance, politics, business (yes, there is a *Newsletter on Newsletters*), employment, food, religions, research, medicine, transportation, taxes, health, recreation and the environment.

You could charge subscribers for your newsletter—annual subscription rates run from a couple of dollars to a couple of thousand dollars (publishers tend to charge whatever the market will bear). If you charge enough for your newsletter, you probably won't need advertising revenue. On the other hand, you could charge a substantial amount for advertising (either classified or display advertising) and give the newsletters away.

If you bring so much advertising into a paid newsletter that it takes up considerable space, you may find you're really publishing a small magazine. Fine. They sell too.

The advantages of a newsletter over a magazine include timeliness, brevity, simplicity of design, and the fact that inside information is provided to a more select audience.

Start a newsletter or magazine devoted solely to classifieds. You could orient it to barter. Or offer a TV listings magazine to be given away free at the stores and retail establishments advertising in it.

You could mimeograph your newsletter (a very inexpensive process) or you could have it printed at any quick-copy shop. Type up your copy with an ordinary typewriter (preferably one with a carbon ribbon). Design (or have designed) a classy masthead. You could have the mastheads printed en masse (like stationery), and mimeo the date and the news portion of the letter.

Promote your newsletter through the mail and with advertising in newspapers and magazines which reach the same people who should be reading your newsletter.

Once you have a newsletter, you can use it to promote any of your other businesses. Hold conferences. Insert ads for your mail-order business. Offer reprints of articles, or sell books or other newsletters. The possibilities a newsletter offers are solely up to your imagination.

TO FIND OUT MORE:

COSMEP (Committee of Small Magazine Editors and Publishers, Box 703, San Francisco, CA 94101) is the trade association for publishers of small literary and poetry magazines.

The Do-It-Yourself Guide to Alternative Publishing (edited by Ron Lichty, Alternative Press Syndicate, Box 777, Cooper Station, New York, NY 10003, 1976) is probably the best book ever compiled on publishing. An 86-page, fully illustrated manual, it tells you everything you need to know to start and run a successful publication: raising capital, choosing a printer, staff organization, design techniques, editing, and much more. Although written from the viewpoint of the alternative press, the information here can be used to start any kind of publication.

The Alternative Press Syndicate (Box 777, Cooper Station, New York, NY 10003) is a nonprofit worldwide association of over 200 alternative newspapers and magazines that began as the Underground Press Syndicate in 1966. There's a one-time fee of $25 for publications to join; after that all services are free, including its magazine, *The Alternative Media Revue*, listings in ad directories, microfilming, exchanges, publicity and news. It's a must for alternative publications. Write for a free brochure. Be sure to enclose a little information about yourself.

The Newsletter on Newsletters (2626 Pennsylvania Ave., N.W., Washington, DC 20037) provides valuable tips and advice for newsletter publishers.

=112=
DESIGN GREETING CARDS

Designing, printing, selling and distributing greeting cards is a field with a wide range of opportunities, limited primarily by your ability to write greetings which turn others on.

Major greeting card companies such as Hallmark turn out four-color-process cards which sell for 25¢ or 35¢; they can sell expensively printed cards cheaply because they turn out thousands of each card.

Don't let their designs limit yours. Ashleigh Brilliant in Santa Barbara has designed hundreds of Pot-Shots postcards. On one side is a hand-lettered message with a simple illustration, all printed in black on the multi-colored cards; on the other side is plenty of space for name and address, stamp and your own message—as well as an advertising message of Brilliant's: In small print, the card notes that there are hundreds of Pot-Shot cards and that, if you can't find them at your local store, you can get a start set and a catalog for $1 from Brilliant Enterprises. The cards are sold widely in head shops.

Specialty groups such as blacks, marijuana smokers, Christians and other religious groups, political organizations, tourists, and occupational groups are often the market targets of card publishers. Marketing possibilities include stores, club fundraisers, and restaurants and hotels.

Probably the two ideal skills to have for this field are the abilities to write pithy statements and to draw (though not necessarily well).

OTHER IDEAS:

Design and market stationery, calendars, posters and bumper stickers.
Sell personalized greeting cards, imprinted to order.
Hand-block-print greeting cards.

TO FIND OUT MORE:

The Art and Craft of Greeting Cards (by Susan Evarts, Northlight Publishers, Westport, CT, 1975) is oriented to exceptionally creative card designs as well as a myriad of methods for producing and reproducing your cards.

How to Make Your Own Greeting Cards (by John Carlis, Watson-Guptill Publications, 1968) is a real idea book: It's intended for individuals who want to send personalized cards. It will provide a great number of commercial ideas, too.

Writing and Selling Greeting Card Verse (by June Barr, The Writer, Inc., 1969) is aimed at writers who want to sell verse to greeting card companies, but also has value for the person about to set up a card company of his/her own.

⫸113⫷
LECTURER

If you have an area of expertise and speak well, you can earn a living lecturing.

Poets regularly traverse the U.S., their travels paid for by the small honorariums they charge universities and schools for readings.

One fellow who had worked for the Underground Press Syndicate for two years toured high schools and college journalism classes to talk about the underground press, bringing copies of dozens of underground papers with him to pique his audience's curiosity.

A Colorado man who designs alternative energy systems lectures (and acts as a consultant) on the subject throughout the West. A California man, nicknamed "Jerusalem John," talks to Jewish groups across the U.S. about Middle Eastern and Judaic history. A Philadelphia man tells audiences about the Aquarian Age, communes and collectives, alternative energies, natural birth control, and mind and faith healing.

Approach local groups in person. Send others a brochure on yourself, listing your qualifications, perhaps with a photo of you giving your rap somewhere. Tack on a cover letter telling them when you'll be in their area, that you'd like to speak, and that you expect an honorarium (a fee).

Many professional lecturers hire lecture-booking agencies to set up their tours. The agencies take commissions on each paid engagement they arrange.

OTHER IDEAS:

Present slide shows, illustrated lectures or travelogues.
Hold workshops.
Be a master of ceremonies or toastmaster.

TO FIND OUT MORE:

Talent (The International Platform Assn., 2564 Berkshire Rd., Cleveland, OH 44106) offers lecturing how-to's, as well as several speeches from famous members of IPA. Since members have included every U.S. President since Teddy Roosevelt, IPA is selective about members—you must be recommended by a present member in your community.

The Speech Writing Guide (by James J. Welsh, John Wiley & Sons, Inc., 1968) instructs the speechwriter and speechgiver on developing a lean speech with humor and style.

How to Write and Deliver a Speech (by John Ott, Trident Press, 1970) is written by a guy who learned speech-writing the hard way—from scratch, ghosting for his boss—and offers considerable expertise in writing the speech.

114
PROFESSIONAL STUDENT

Being a professional student takes a certain knack for school and a willingness to deal with institutions. Bureaucrats often will not volunteer information that you need in order to pursue

grants and scholarships, so you may have to search out information that you need. Of course, if you don't like school, this is
not a good situation for you.

There are many sources of income for students. State and
federal governments grant scholarships based on academic qualifications and need. There are scholarships for veterans and their
children, and Social Security and vocational rehab scholarships
for the handicapped, their children, and the children of deceased
parents; other agencies grant scholarships to minority groups.
Many clubs, unions, foundations and corporations grant scholarships and assistance awards.

Graduate students receive grants, fellowships, residencies,
teaching grants, loans (many of which are forgiven under certain circumstances), and contracts for research.

There are also opportunities in technical areas. Scholarships
and grants, usually lasting between six months and two years,
are sometimes offered to people training in many areas, including health services (medic, nurse, paramedic), drafting, engineering and other design fields, and technical computer work.

Mike Fried has earned his second masters degree. He had
received a National Defense Scholarship in biology and a sup-
plemental award from his mother's union. Mike finds science a
consuming interest. "I consider all the sciences a hobby. . . .
Courses are regimenting but they are an external source of dis-
cipline."

When Mike graduated he found the job market overcrowded.
He decided to stay in school. He is currently enrolled in a Ph.D.
program, with a teaching fellowship. When he graduates he plans
to do postgraduate studies in genetic engineering.

Janice Roberts earned a Ph.D. in languages from the University of California, Santa Cruz. "When I looked for work I was
told that I was overqualified. I went back to the school and
found a fellowship offered to Americans willing to do postgraduate work on Malaysia and its culture. It's a two-year grant,
eighteen months of it in Malaysia.

"I don't know what I'll do when it runs out, but I've been in school twenty-one years now. I guess I'll last it out—I'm scared of the outside world."

Students talk about the tremendous amount of free time that they have. Many programs encourage independent research, so that the student's time is his/her own. "As long as you get all the work done they don't care how much time you spend at it." They like the long vacations, frequent holidays, and informal life of the campus.

But there are some disadvantages to the field. The income can be low—some scholarships are for small cash sums. Many people consider the school system oppressive. Other people feel that they have developed a distorted world view from interacting only with other students and teachers for so long.

OTHER IDEAS:

Various voluntary and government agencies offer grants to individuals for specific research in various fields. For instance, a woman in Fresno, California, won a grant to find out how the police can improve their sensitivity to victims of assault and rape.

TO FIND OUT MORE:

Annual Register of Grant Support (ed. by Deanna Sclar and the staff of Academic Media, Orange, NJ) is over 800 pages of fellowships and grant support programs available from government agencies, foundations, and business and professional organizations. A comprehensive, up-to-date, authoritative reference work.

How to Get Money for Education: Fellowships and Scholarships (compiled by Stephen E. Nowlan et al., Chilton Books, Radnor, PA, 1975) is for a much broader readership than just college students, which could make it more valuable. It covers funding sources for fellowships and scholarships, as well as fundraising and proposal writing.

208

The College Blue Book: Scholarships, Fellowships, Grants and Loans (ed. by M. Lorraine Mathies, Macmillan, 1975) is the list of hundreds and hundreds of sources for college money. Well compiled.

=115=
DESIGN/MURAL/ WALL SCENE PAINTER

Painting designs, murals, and wall scenes on indoor walls is a field which is growing as more and more people get involved with creating home "environments."

One New York artist specializes in painting rooms sky blue (all four walls, ceiling, and floor), then adding clouds with spray paint and rainbows with brush and roller.

Another artist creates Art Deco designs and wall art with paint, aluminum foil and tape.

Still other artists transform rooms into sunsets, grassy pastures or thunderstorms, or copy famous drawings or favorite photographs.

To sell others on your indoor schemes, you may wish to create them first in your own home or apartment. Show potential clients what you can do—and go from there.

You need create a design only once, if you draw it on a sheet of graph paper. When you go to the wall, draw the same graph on the wall in a larger scale.

Outdoor walls are usually the sides of buildings. Sometimes you can convince a store owner to pay for an outdoor wall mural as advertising. Or dun all the merchants up and down the street. Apply for grant monies to pay for your work (see "Fund-raising"), as many artists have done in urban neighborhoods. Or put out a donation can while you paint (the note on the can might say, "Project Supported Solely by Your Contributions") —a Berkeley collective raised $800 that way and drew support from the community as well.

OTHER IDEAS:

Specialize in creating environments in kids' rooms, offices, commercial buildings, lobbies, bedrooms or living rooms.

Offer your services to restaurants and stores. Commercial spaces are often painted in dramatic styles.

Build designs on walls using burlap, wood shingles, or other materials.

Use spray foam to create a design and insulate a building or room at the same time.

Hang scenic wallpaper.

TO FIND OUT MORE:

Mural Manual: How to Paint Murals for the Classroom, Community Center, and Street Corner (by Mark Rogovin, intro. by Pete Seeger, Beacon Press, 1975) is how-to all the way—finding sites, getting permissions, sketches, walls, finances, publicity, portable murals, etc.

Street Art. (by Robert Sommer, Links, 1975) is a beautiful book which will give the street and mural artist dozens of ideas. Fine (wall) art, children's (wall) art, art on outhouses, roadside sculpture, rock art, oil field art, etc. Discussion of each.

116
CONSULTANT

Being a consultant is almost as easy as being a lecturer, but in this case, you're selling your expertise to a business.

Small businesspeople are constantly getting involved in new products or new market areas they're not really familiar with. If you've got the answers to their questions, most small businesspersons will either pay you or give you a piece of their company.

Profit-making companies utilize only a fraction of the consulting market. Nonprofits, government agencies, individuals, churches, lawyers and other professional people, consumers, and students all make use of paid consultants.

To get business: Keep in touch with the business community in your area; watch for new products or services you feel need improvement; listen for news of new companies forming to produce goods or services with which you are familiar.

OTHER IDEAS:

Lead seminars and organize intraoffice educational training sessions.

═══ 117 ═══
FREELANCE WRITER/EDITOR

You can earn money writing newspaper and magazine articles, books, brochures and pamphlets for businesses and organizations, advertising copy for businesses, as-told-to books, travel folders, company newsletters, booklets, jokes, greeting-card copy, family histories, speeches, public relations releases, store promotions, and cartoon gags.

You can earn money editing book manuscripts, dissertations and newsletters.

To get local writing and editing work, put together a portfolio of the work you've done, and then advertise in the local journals' classifieds, on bulletin boards, etc., that you're available at reasonable prices.

And you'll probably have more business than you know what to do with.

TO FIND OUT MORE:

Your Personal Column (by J.B. Hunter, Creative Book Co., P.O. Box 214998, Sacramento, CA 95821) suggests some compelling reasons to write a column and gives some good advice on going about it.

Stranger Than Naked; or How to Write Dirty Books for Fun and Profit: A Manual (by Mike McGrady, Peter H. Wyden, Inc., 1970) is an amusing book on writing "big money" books. McGrady masterminded one of the most profitable literary hoaxes of all time: *Naked Came the Stranger* was written by 24 Long Island newspaper reporters and editors under one pseudonym and became a sexy bestseller.

How to Make Money Writing Magazine Articles (ed. by Beatrice Schapper with the Society of Magazine Writers, Arco, 1974) takes eight articles by freelance professionals, and then has the authors explain how they put the article together, blow-by-blow, from the first glimmer of the idea. A valuable work.

Writing Articles That Sell (by Louise Boggess, Prentice-Hall, 1965) offers valuable insight into the process of writing salable articles.

The Art of Readable Writing (by Rudolf Flesch, Collier, 1972) will teach you to write more clearly and effectively. *Time* called Flesch the "Mr. Fix-It of Writing."

Writer's Market (Writer's Digest, 9933 Alliance Road, Cincinnati, OH 45242; annual) lists *thousands* of markets for freelance articles, photos, poems, fillers and books.

The Complete Guide to Editorial Freelancing (by Carol L. O'Neill and Avina Ruder, Dodd, Mead, 1974) is *invaluable*.

══ 118 ══
PRODUCE A RADIO SHOW

Radio stations hire people to host shows, and to sell radio advertisements or air time.

If you are skilled but would like to work for yourself, try producing your own radio show. Convince one or more advertisers that it is in their best interests to advertise on the show you plan to produce (i.e., sell them). And convince a radio station that it is in its best interests to air your show—that you can offer a sponsor, a larger audience, more profit for the time you're on the air, or some combination of the three.

You can produce a show you don't host. Hire someone to do the hosting. The Federal Communications Commission sets standards, including first- and third-class radio licenses, for those who host and engineer most radio shows, so check its requirements.

Two women in San Francisco developed a 13-week half-hour Jewish children's show to be aired one summer. They persuaded a public education station to play the show. Then they persuaded one of the Jewish agencies in town to fund the show through a $1000 grant.

OTHER IDEAS:

Syndicate a show and get paid by several stations. Or syndicate it by being paid by advertisers and giving your formatted show, complete with advertisements, to the stations free (called "barter syndication").

Sell tapes and transcripts of your show to your listeners. Turn the transcripts of your guests' comments into a book.

TO FIND OUT MORE:

Broadcast Operator Handbook (by the Federal Communications Commission, Supt. of Documents, U.S. Government Printing Office, Washington, DC 20402, #004-000-00329-2) is a study manual to obtain a Radiotelephone Third Class Operators Permit with the endorsement to operate broadcast radio stations. It's amazingly well written—you almost wouldn't know it's a government publication.

═══ 119 ═══
INVENTOR

Inventing new products and improvements on old products can be exciting and profitable. Only a small percentage of inventors earns money at it. Successful inventors are ones who can visualize not only new concepts but also commercial modes of marketing them.

Should you decide to market an invention, carefully follow the procedures for patent search (to be sure you're the first to patent your idea) and a patent application. The patent protects the financial value of your invention.

You may want to market your invention to someone equipped to manufacture your product, for some combination of cash and royalties—or you may wish to market the product yourself, and turn from inventing to manufacturing as your means to earn a living without working for someone else.

OTHER IDEAS:

Make or publicize others' inventions. Kurt Saxon publishes *The Survivor*, a magazine composed mostly of reprints of old *Popular Mechanics* magazine how-to articles for building "appropriate technology" machinery. Perhaps one of these inventions could be made or sold in your community.

Some "New Age" inventors have been licensing their technology to companies which manufacture only for distribution to their localities. One stove manufacturer, licensed by just such an inventor, said, "There is always room for a better wood-burning stove."

TO FIND OUT MORE:

California has an Inventors Council (P.O. Box 376, San Francisco, CA 94101) which provides information on clearing, protecting and marketing new products.

Invention development companies sprang up in response to the needs of inventors to get their innovations hustled to the companies which might buy them. Note, though, that many of these companies charge initial fees to the inventor. So they encourage almost every inventor, despite the improbabilities of market success for some products.

The Raymond Lee Organization, Inc. (230 Park Ave., New York, NY 10017), for example, claims to be one of the largest invention-development companies, and says that 1001 corporations review each new product idea as it becomes available. Its Inventor's Kit is free to any person with an invention idea.

Your invention can be marketed through a trade show: Patent Expositions across the country are run by Patexpo, Exposition Management, International New Products Center, 680 Fifth Ave., New York, NY 10019. A booth will cost several hundred dollars to display your invention to the tens of thousands of prospective buyers who are said to attend.

United Inventors and Scientists (14431 Chase St., Panorama City, CA 91402) is a nonprofit member organization for inventors, scientists and small businesspeople, offering marketing information and services, a pre-patent protection service, and a newsletter.

Inventors Workshop International (121 N. Fir St., Ventura, CA 93001) is a nonprofit membership organization which has set up a step-by-step program to help member inventors take their ideas through the various stages of protection, development, manufacturing and, finally, marketing. It publishes a magazine, *LightBulb*, a handbook and a journal. The organization also offers patent searches; a telephone chain for important information; a hotline; and annual Inventors Expos to generate buyer interest.

How to Be a Successful Inventor: Patenting, Protecting, Marketing and Selling Your Invention (by Clarence R. Taylor, Exposition Press, 1972) points out, "Imagination and inventive-ess are not uncommon. What *is* uncommon is the ability to get a new idea, demonstrated in a device or process, to market. That is what this book is about."

Inventors Project Book (by L. George Lawrence, Howard W. Sams & Co., 1971) offers a great deal of helpful information to the inventor, and suggests 120 problems for which inventions are needed (e.g., onion peeler, golf trainer).

Complete Guide to Making Money with Your Ideas and Inventions (by Richard E. Paige, Prentice-Hall, 1973) tells the prospective inventor to stick to areas about which she/he knows, suggests how to be on the lookout for opportunities, points out how inventions can make money, and counsels readers on selling and marketing and merchandising techniques to bring in the bucks. Straightforward advice worth the reading.

Inventors Source Book: How to Turn Ideas into Inventions (by Susan N. Hartman and Norman C. Parrish, Inventors Resource Center, P.O. Box 5105, 2901 College Ave., Berkeley, CA 94705, 1975) takes the inventor through the paces—ideas, brainstorming, evaluation, patents, profits, and where to get even more help.

120
PRODUCE RECORDS

Producing records can be fun, risky, profitable, heady, and a lot of hard work.

The People's Victory Orchestra and Chorus in New York City produced its own album and its own 45-rpm record a few years ago. Members did their own promotion and their own distribution. It was a small success, paying for itself plus part of the time spent on it.

A Webster City, Iowa, band bussed to Chicago, taped a session, and then cut a 45-rpm record. The band's manager gave free copies of the record to Iowa radio stations, and persuaded Iowa record stores to carry it. Sales were high enough to pay for the Chicago trip as well as the manager's time. And the record promoted the band's appearances around the state.

Producing records offers big profits if the band becomes a hit or if the record has some kind of lasting value. You could try both: produce records for bands you feel will last and grow popular; and produce records which teach (Morse Code, languages, etc.) or which capture a culture (such as the Folkways record catalog, which includes among its titles "Mushroom Ceremony of the Mazatec Indians of Mexico," Canyon Records' "Peyote Songs" or Elektra's "Authentic Sound Effects").

Figure each record will cost 50¢ or so if you do 1000 or more copies. Jackets could cost from 5¢ to 50¢ each. Most of the record-pressing plants are located in metropolitan areas, particularly Los Angeles; you'll get a better deal if you deal with the plant directly rather than going through a local broker. Give your artists royalties of 10 to 15 percent of sales.

OTHER IDEAS:

Produce records of religious singers to be sold, not in stores, but at each church visited and each concert given. Popular local groups sometimes sell their records at concerts and recitals, a practice established especially in folk-music circles. Even classical ensemblists have sold records at concert tour locations. For various fees, you provide or book the studio, mix the tapes, and direct and inspect record plant production and jacketing.

TO FIND OUT MORE:

Star-Making Machinery: The Odyssey of an Album (by Geoffrey Stokes, Bobbs-Merrill, 1975) will give you a thorough sense of how it's done in the big-time. There's no encouragement for small-time producers, but reading between the lines should give you a feeling for where you might fit in.

Diane Rapaport and her company Music Works (Box 838, San Rafael, CA, 94902) are putting together a book to be titled *Music Works—A Guide to Making and Selling Your Own Records,* as well as their magazine, *Music Works—a Manual for Musicians,* a semi-annual bible for performers and managers. An excellent value.

121
INTERIOR DECORATOR

Interior decorating requires creativity plus. If you like decorating, begin with your own home.

One Connecticut woman who loves creating environments and moods got into interior decorating just that way—and discovered she could finish her own home at a discount and attract business at the same time.

For clients, start with friends, neighbors, relatives and acquaintances. If they like the moods and the flavors or the environment you created, they may wish to hire you to do their homes.

Interior decorators get wholesale discounts on furniture, materials, drapes, and other home accessories. And they sell at retail.

You will probably want to learn techniques and tricks through interior decorating courses. There are also many books and magazines published in the field. It may be useful to develop your sketching ability, as well.

OTHER IDEAS:

Manufacture your own furniture, draperies, art objects, etc., for a higher share of the profits.

Try charging a small fee for home advisory visits, paying for most of your time with your percentage on the furnishings you sell.

TO FIND OUT MORE:

The American Society of Interior Designers (730 Fifth Ave., New York, NY 10019) is a professional association. It publishes an "Interior Design Career Guide" which places heavy emphasis on graduating from a recognized three-year professional school of interior design. Decide for yourself.

122
INVESTOR

If you own money, and are careful, you can make more by investing it.

You can invest in stocks and bonds. See a broker.

You can also invest your money in people with good ideas who you believe can make a profit with the help of some seed capital.

Some of the ideas in this book require more capital than some of the readers of this book will have. For example, running an emotional or physical conditioning center could be extremely profitable, but requires a sizable investment in equipment.

As an investor, your task would be to find a partner compatible with the business to risk his or her time and your money to start and run the business.

Have your lawyer draw up a contract giving you a permanent percentage of the profits (assuming, of course, that the business succeeds) and dividing control of the company in some way between you and your partner.

You may want to help out and do actual work in the early days of the company. Later, if the business works out, you can lie back and collect the fruits of your invested capital.

TO FIND OUT MORE:

The Money Game (by Adam Smith, Random House, 1968) offers a good understanding of money, who wins, who loses, and why.

⑫③
ALTERNATIVE MEDICINE

It's illegal to practice medicine without a license. But alternative medical practitioners are being held in renewed respect by Americans. The number of healers, herbologists, acupuncturists, iridologists and midwives is on the rise.

Midwives say they are helping mothers who want to deliver at home. They say doctors oppose home deliveries; having midwives there makes the practice safer. Should complications arise, they call in doctors to help.

Herbologists are healers who recommend natural medicines for curing illness. They may also be in the retail herb business.

Acupuncture and acupressure are healing techniques which make use of various sensitive points along the body.

There are many other holistic health techniques which do not rely on drug therapy.

These are learned arts of responsibility. You are taking another person's health into your hands. Training and a sober sense about your work are required.

=124=
ARTIST/PAINTER/ SCULPTOR

Becoming a fine artist takes years of work, developing techniques and learning the art of self-expression. On the other hand, first works on every level can also be sold, if marketed properly.

One young developing artist sells his ballpoint pen drawings —they're quite good, very intricate—for a dollar apiece at flea markets.

Another artist has set up newspaper vending machines on street corners to vend "drawings of the week" for 50¢; he says he wants to bring the works of struggling young artists like himself directly to people where they live and work.

Other artists find patrons who may even house and feed them while they develop their art (some artist-patron relationships combine art and sex—see chapter 29, "Kept Man/Kept Woman").

Only a small percentage of those who try the fine arts are able to earn a living from them. Some artists also teach art or sell commercial artwork (magazine and book art, for example).

It's not easy to get one of the big commercial galleries to take on your work, and they often take what seem like enormous sales commissions. Nevertheless, a great many young artists still aim for the chance to affiliate with such a gallery.

A number of Wyoming artists and sculptors who are earning a living at it show their works in various small galleries and shops around the state. And an Iowa woman I know who is becoming well known and liked for her paintings on weathered barn wood places her work for sale in restaurants as well as galleries and shows. She does quite well.

OTHER IDEAS:

Paint business or organization posters.

Exhibit and sell work in art stores, banks, galleries, museums, restaurants, shopping malls, hotel and motel lobbies, community centers, showings in your own home, outdoor art shows and community bazaars, architects' offices, corporate lobbies, big building lobbies (make sure there's security), doctors' offices, church foyers, sidewalk shows and furniture stores.

Paint pet portraits.

Turn blueprints into paintings of the future buildings for real-estate developers and architects.

TO FIND OUT MORE:

Artists Market (annual; edited by Kirk Polking and Liz Prince, Writer's Digest, 9933 Alliance Rd., Cincinnati, OH 45242) is invaluable, containing sample commissioned art agreements; samples of art, cartoons, crafts and photos purchased by the various markets listed; interviews with reps and buyers; 2800 markets; and helpful suggestions on how to get to them effectively.

125
PUBLISHING

To produce books as an agent or publisher, you need a honed sense of the commercial—of what will sell.

There are many steps to producing a book: Brainstorming book ideas, finding the right author, editing work and preparing the manuscript, typesetting the book, designing the cover or jacket, and bidding out the printing and binding jobs (or doing them yourself).

The final step, distribution, is crucial. Without visibility, no product can sell. Stores are often reluctant to carry books by small publishers. But there is always room for another publisher with good products and aggressive marketing. Many independent book publishers contract for distribution with a large publishing house or with a group such as Book People, a Berkeley book distribution cooperative.

OTHER IDEAS:

Produce a game. San Francisco State University professor Ralph Anspach sold nearly half a million copies of his game, Anti-Monopoly, over four years before he was forced by the makers of Monopoly to change the name of his game. Now it's called Anti.

Publish calendars.

Be a publishing consultant. Help people publish their own books.

TO FIND OUT MORE:

COSMEP—The Committee of Small Magazine Editors and Publishers (P.O. Box 703, San Francisco, CA 94101)—is for the folks who put out small and alternative-press publications. COSMEP has a mobile bookstore traversing the country, publishes a regular newsletter, holds conferences, and publishes a handbook with sections on distribution, library and bookstore sales, promotion, production, printing, and finances. It also has library and bookstore lists available in label form.

Friends of Books and Comics (330 Ellis St., San Francisco, CA 94102) maintains an excellent mailing list which it uses and which also makes its way into the hands of all kinds of people whose resources you could find valuable. It supports and encourages small presses. When you're ready to begin producing books, be sure to write to tell them what you're doing and to get on the mailing list.

Literary Market Place: Directory of American Book Publishing (annual; R. R. Bowker Co.) lists everything to do with book publishing, including agents, art, direct mail promotion, bookbinding and printing. Study it.

The Publish-It-Yourself Handbook (ed. by Bill Henderson, Pushcart Press, Box 845, Yonkers, NY 10701, 1973) combines a whole lot of "how-we-published-our-own-books" stories with some practical suggestions. Inspirational.

Publicizing Your Self-Published Book (by Herman Blackey, Creative Book Co., P.O. Box 214998, Sacramento, CA 95821, 1976) is super. You can do exactly what the title says—and it provides the necessary instruction as well as enough ideas to animate your creativity.

How to Self Publish Your Own Book and Make It a Best Seller (by Ted Nicholas, Enterprise Publishing Co., 1300 Market St., Wilmington, DE 19801, 1975): This book is printed in manuscript form—typed and double-spaced, instead of type-set. That made it much cheaper to produce, but (for me at least) much harder to read. Nevertheless, it covers the field—the business aspects of publishing, which many authors tend to ignore, are covered particularly well.

Into Print (by Mary Hill and Wendell Cochran, William Kaufman Inc., Los Altos, CA, 1977) is very good. Its sample forms (for getting permissions, for example) are very helpful.

=====================126=====================
FREELANCE PHOTOGRAPHER

For millions of Americans, photography is a gratifying hobby— one which they enjoy, which gives them permanent memories, and which they'd spend much more time at if they had the spare time and money to devote to it. If you're a photo bug, you may as well take photographs for money—and do what you enjoy for a living.

One of the ways to make a living with your camera is to sell photographs of news events to the local newspaper, the Associated Press, or United Press International. When a New York radical was arrested for allegedly plotting to bomb the Capitol in Washington a few years ago, an amateur photographer in New York City had the only known photographs of the woman—and even better, in one of his photos she was draped in the American flag. They brought a good price from a news syndicate. Another amateur in Sydney, Australia, earned over $1000 from a news syndicate. He'd been dinking around at the airport, snapping pix of planes landing and taking off. From one of the planes taking off, a stowaway who'd been hidden in the wheel housing fell to his death. The amateur had the picture.

The key to news photography is taking your camera with you wherever you go. News organizations have staff photographers to send to events—but they don't have enough photographers to have one stationed everywhere a news event might happen. Use a 35mm camera with Tri-X film (black and white); both are standard, and thus make for easy developing.

Know your camera, so that you can take pictures accurately when the news develops quickly. And once you've got shots you think are newsworthy, get to a phone—quickly—and call a news photo editor. The more quickly you can get your photographs to a news organization which wants them, the more valuable they are. The paper or syndicate will do the processing. Payment, when a sale is made, will range from $5 to $5000, depending on how much demand there is for your photos. And if your photo has national news possibilities, call AP or UPI before your local or state newspaper. Use your photo sales to get to know staffers, and you may be able to wangle freelance assignments when extra photographers are needed.

Photographers are also hired to shoot or film weddings, confirmations, parties, new babies, children, families, pets and businesses. The trickiest, of course, is weddings—they only happen once—and if you forgot to load film in your camera, you're going to have half a town angry with you. Before you tackle weddings, be sure you have the equipment you need and be sure you know your stuff.

Country clubs and fraternities often hire photographers for their parties. In some cases, the fraternity brother agrees to pay $2 (or whatever) for the picture of himself and his date (cash could even be required in advance). In other cases, the photographer is paid by the house or club to take pictures of everyone who requests it. Each picture comes finished in a frame (which could be inexpensive or not).

To take pictures of children, families or pets, you may want to have a studio. Or, in the case of children, you may take the photos in familiar surroundings around their homes. If you can capture kids on film, you are liable to be called upon often—and previous photographs will sell future ones. It takes spontaneity—and a lot of it—to get expression out of kids.

It will take some selling to persuade most businesses to buy your photographic skills. Pictures of various hair styles might help a hair stylist in his business. Or how about before and after shots for a roofer, an aluminum-sider or a landscape artist? Industrial photographs are the bread and butter of many freelance photographers—often industries can save money by using slide shows for training. The post office, for example, has a slide show on dogs and dog bites which is required viewing for all mail carriers.

If you attend local events, sell pictures of participants to the individual or his or her family. One Wyoming school teacher, Red Grosgebauer, started photographing rodeos in his spare time. A year later he was doing it full-time. He traveled from rodeo to rodeo in his camper-pickup, with his chemicals and tanks and enlarger. He'd take photographs one day and have them available for sale the next. He took at least one picture of every rodeo participant, and blew up every negative into an 8x10 print. If the rodeo was over the following day, he took the remainder of the photos to the local saddle store—since people coming in to buy photographs often also purchased rodeo supplies from the store, the owners didn't even charge a commission on the prints, which sold for $3.

Another photographic possibility is vacation spots. When you ride up the ski lift on Snow King Mountain in Jackson, Wyoming, a photographer snaps your picture (the background is breathtaking). He shows each person what the picture will look like by showing a shot he's already had developed from a previous day. He takes their money and agrees to send the picture as soon as it's printed.

Bear Mountain State Park in upstate New York is a favorite day trip for many New York City residents. When you rent a paddle-boat, a photographer offers to take your picture in the boat with Bear Mountain as the backdrop. If you agree, when you return from paddling around the lake, she has your picture mounted in a key chain for you to take with you.

To take pictures in a resort area, consider what tourists will think is most memorable. It might be a shot with Mount Rushmore in the background. Or it might be under the marquee at Radio City Music Hall. If a resort is involved, you may have to make a deal with the resort owner, the management or the park service—you may have to pay them rent or a commission on every sale. If you've chosen the right spot, it will be worth it— over and over again.

OTHER IDEAS:

A company in Atlanta, Georgia, started by a camera enthusiast shoots product and factory stills for company brochures.

Another woman photographs houses for real-estate agents.

A 60-year-old Vermont photographer sells scenic photo Christmas cards to fraternal organizations for resale. Other photographers produce family picture greeting cards and postcards (photo-paper cards are available at many camera stores).

Exhibit your photos in galleries, museums, photo shops, banks, shopping malls, hotel and motel lobbies, community centers and bazaars, sidewalk shows and corporate lobbies. Offer commissions if they sell.

A photographer in Detroit photographs homes and their contents for home and fire insurance purposes. Picture documentation can help the homeowner or renter remember exactly what he or she owned before the fire or theft, and provide proof of condition for negotiations with insurance companies.

A St. Louis photographer shoots pets. He finds customers at animal shows and through local pet clubs and kennels.

An Iowa photographer shoots each high-school graduate during commencement exercises, and shows and sells the prints to the proud parents and grandparents.

Some photo buffs specialize in restoration of old prints. One photo restorer working in Harlem says that his business has quadrupled since *Roots* because of renewed interest in family history and background.

Many amateur photographers would prefer to develop their own photos but do not have money or space to set up their own darkrooms. Several photographers we know around the country rent their darkroom space and equipment during their off hours. They find it very profitable.

Specialize in photographing artwork. Sell pictures to the artist, the gallery or museum, art dealers, collectors, universities and art institutions.

TO FIND OUT MORE:

Artist's and Photographer's Market (annual; Writer's Digest, 9933 Alliance Road, Cincinnati, OH 45242) lists thousands of markets for freelance photos.

Introduction to Photography (by Robert B. Rhode and Floyd H. McCall, Macmillan, 1971) is used in many college photojournalism courses and is an excellent guide to good photography.

Freelance Magazine Photography (by Lou Jacobs Jr., Hastings House, 1965, 1970) provides an excellent introduction to freelance photojournalism, for advertising agencies and book publishers as well as for magazines. It offers advice for beginners, briefly covers legal position, and has lots of how-to.

How to Make Money with Your Camera (by Ted Schwarz, H.P. Books, P.O. Box 5367, Tucson, AZ 85703, 1974) is a fine idea book with dozens of ways to make money with your camera.

Professional Photographers of America, Inc. (1090 Executive Way, Oak Leaf Commons, Des Plaines, IL 60018) provides members with the monthly *Professional Photographer* magazine, newsletters, handbooks, seminars, workshops, wedding and graduation promotion kits, business consulting, standard business forms, a public relations kit, and advertising and sales promotion. It also runs the Winona School of Professional Photography.

The Society of Photographers in Communications—known as ASMP—(60 E. 42 St., New York, NY 10017)—is a tremendous organization. It has established minimum rates and standards (its complete guide to photo pricing—*ASMP Guide to Business Practices in Photography*—is free to members, $5 to others); it negotiates with publishers and ad agencies, and much, much more. ASMP is well respected. It publishes a monthly bulletin and a membership directory.

Popular Photography (One Park Ave., New York, NY 10016) periodically spotlights a photographer who is making a living in some aspect of the art.

Photography Market Place (ed. by Fred W. McDarrah, R. R. Bowker Co.; annual) is a sourcebook to picture buyers (in 11 categories), technical services, equipment sources, supportive services, picture sources, publishers and publications of photography, organizations, and career opportunities. It is a series of lists of sources; it makes no suggestions on how to get access to or use them.

Opportunities in Photography Careers (by Bervin M. Johnson, Vocational Guidance Manuals, Universal, 235 E. 45 St., New York, NY, 10017, 1969) is one of the best of the guidance genre. Check it out; it has many good ideas.

The Photography Catalog (ed. by Norman Snyder, Harper & Row, 1976) provides access to shooting and darkroom equipment, basic how-to, books, magazines, schools, films, unusual processes and techniques, and careers. And its collection of photos will provide hours and hours of ideas.

═127═
LOW-BUDGET MOVIE/
VIDEO PRODUCER

In San Francisco, Janet Sluizer teamed up with a video porta-pack man and produced an hour-long documentary on marijuana which was shown on cable TV in San Francisco and New York and which is being syndicated elsewhere. It cost the two less than $100.

The Yippies in New York produce their own weekly cable TV show; they find advertising sponsors to pay the cost.

Pink Flamingos and *Female Trouble* are widely recognized as two of the grossest movies ever produced—which is exactly what brought big boxoffice returns. Starring a transvestite named Divine, each was produced for under $50,000.

It's very easy to spend a fortune in the film world. It requires far more creative planning to bring in your film for less.

Many nature documentaries—shot for television or for viewing in high schools, colleges and lecture halls—are low-budget films.

If you're good at both film producing and at hustling money, you may be able to do what Barbara Kopple did. Her feature-length documentary, *Harlan County USA,* won an Academy Award in 1977; Kopple had scrounged nearly $400,000—a mere pittance by Hollywood standards—while spending three years producing and directing her documentary about coal-mining life in southeastern Kentucky.

You may want to begin your career in film and video by recording private events—weddings, births, confirmations, family reunions, etc.—to let your customers relive the special moments of their lives over and over again.

TO FIND OUT MORE:

Currently, a Film Fund for Social Change is being organized in Boston to bring together filmmakers and foundations.

The Canyon (California) Cinema Cooperative claims to be the only West Coast film distributor which welcomes the works of any and all U.S. independent filmmakers.

Educational Film Library Association (43 W. 61 St., New York, NY 10023) serves as a national clearinghouse for information about 16mm films and other non-print media, including their production, distribution and use in education, the arts, science, industry, religion; these last groups make up a good share of the organizational membership. A recent book, *16mm Distribution Handbook,* is especially geared for independent filmmakers, covering all aspects of distribution, including contract negotiations, legal considerations, notes on theater deals, public television markets, global markets, universities, co-ops, etc. Other books include filmographies, manuals and directories. EFLA publishes *Sightlines* five times per year; administers an independent evaluation program to assist film libraries, audiovisual directors and educators in film selection; sponsors the American Film Festival; and holds workshops.

The Film-Makers' Cooperative (175 Lexington Ave., New York, NY 10016) mentioned in Chapter 78 is also a very good way to gain wide public exposure for your films. The Cooperative accepts all films and does not seek exclusive distribution. Filmmakers receive 75 percent of all rentals collected in their behalf. The Cooperative defrays operating costs by the use of 25 percent of rentals collected, plus handling charges assessed to rentors on each rental. They even list other distributors of the same films. They seem to be fine people.

Van Nostrand Reinhold Manual of Film-Making (by Barry Callaghan, Van Nostrand Reinhold Co., 1973) is a front-to-back guidebook to filmmaking for the professional.

Motion Picture Market Place (ed. by Tom Costner, Little, Brown and Co., 1976; annual) is a directory of production, professional talent, services, distribution, agents, equipment, and publicity for film. Invaluable.

128
SPEED READER

Eric is a professional speed reader. He sets up at a table in the coffee and short-order section of Iowa State's Memorial Union on one of the most traveled indoor pathways to ISU classes. His posterboard sign, set on the table where he's sitting, reminds passersby that he'll read any book, and outline it, for only a few dollars.

"I'll read anything but foreign languages and math texts," he says, adding that the concept of getting paid for reading is one he's delighted to have latched onto. "People are actually paying me to read their books for them! I'm learning more than I ever did in any class and I'm being paid for it."

Eric was a student in one of the first of the speed-reading courses. When he started, he was no different from most readers; his reading speed was about 300 to 400 words per minute. Then he excelled in speed reading. He found his mind grasped whole pages of material at a glance, once he'd learned speed-reading techniques; within a few months, he was reading over 10,000 words per minute and returning to teach his former speed-reading instructors a few techniques he'd learned on his own.

Eric's speed-reading profession began as a creative homework assignment: "I thought I could practice and improve my speed-reading skills by reading other people's books for pay; providing them with outlines of the books tested my ability over and over again."

He also gives out business cards with his phone number, and places an occasional classified ad. One fraternity man, hard put to read Faulkner's *Absalom, Absalom,* let alone draw a character analysis from it as a class assignment, called on Eric. In two hours, Eric had read the novel, outlined its plot, and written an analysis of the designated character.

129
REAL-ESTATE BROKER/ADVISOR

Real-estate brokers are usually paid 6 percent of the selling price of the house. A broker can earn a living selling only one home every month or two.

Many real-estate agents specialize. A Southern broker, for example, specializes in land for folks in the back-to-the-land movement. She sends out newsletters with photos of the various parcels available.

A broker in Sausalito, California, specializes in the exotic. He spends his time scaring up South Sea islands and remote forest retreats for customers who want to get away from it all.

Selling and brokering real estate require a state license, which means getting to know state and local rules and regulations to pass a test. You can learn on the job (as a secretary, for example), from books (see your public library), or from a local college course. Your local real-estate board or state real-estate commission can fill you in on requirements for a license.

Real-estate advisors charge fees for advising. "How can we add value to our home with the least expense?" their clients ask. "Where should we buy our home—where will home values rise at least as quickly as inflation? Should we buy a home for ourselves or a duplex or quadriplex for ourselves plus income?" Property buyers ask advisors those questions and more every day.

TO FIND OUT MORE:

The National Association of Realtors (430 N. Michigan Ave., Chicago, IL 60611) says it's the largest trade and professional association in the U.S. The association has registered "realtor" as a trademark, so the word may be used only by professional members of NAR who subscribe to its Code of Ethics. It has established nine affiliated groups, including the American Society of Real Estate Counselors.

The Monopoly Game: The "How To" Book of Making Big Money with Rental Homes and *How to Grow a Moneytree!: The Magical Book of Making Big Money with Second Mortgages* (both by Dave Glubetich, realtor, Glubetich Enterprises, 12 Gregory Lane, Pleasant Hill, CA 94523): If you're advising people about real estate *as an investment* or if you are an investor, both of these books provide solid how-to on real-estate money-making.

How to Go from Rags to Riches Fast with Sound Real Estate Investment (by J. Brad Lampley, Prentice-Hall, 1976) has lots of advice. Use it yourself. Or loan the book to friends to get them to use your brokering services and get into real estate.

The Real Estate Investing Letter (United Media International, Inc., 306 Dartmouth St., Boston, MA 02116) is an eight-page newsletter, filled with in-depth investing advice. You or a client interested in buying houses, apartment buildings, etc., for earnings could find this useful.

=130=
SMALL AIRPLANE PILOT

Getting a private pilot's license costs a thousand dollars, and getting a commercial license costs another thousand. But think of your local air service as a trade school: Commercial pilots have a skill that's in demand.

A used single-engine, two-place plane can cost as little as a thousand or two thousand dollars. For many passenger runs, you'll want twin-engine rating so that you can rent a six- or eight-place plane. Wyoming lawyers hire such planes to take their clients to court across a mountain range in the morning and be back seeing other clients by noon.

Regular cargo can be just about anything, as can special shipments. One private pilot flies flowers from the San Francisco area to New York. Wyoming cities and towns have hired planes to deliver last-minute grant applications to federal agencies in Denver and Salt Lake City.

═ 131 ═
WORK WITH COMPUTERS

We are at the beginning of the Age of Computers. The IBM giants of the early '60's have been condensed into tabletop-size computers through the use of miniaturized electronic circuitry. This miniaturization is still going on. In the near future, hand-held computers the size of today's electronic calculators will be mass-marketed, their prices making them accessible to everyone. Also under development are new measuring tools, new uses for calculators, and more powerful giant processors.

In any expanding market there is room for the adventure-some self-employed as well as for employees. Be a computer programmer, analyst, technician, software designer, hardware designer, or peripheral equipment designer.

A computer engineer/scientist in Illinois designed a compiler program he felt computer hobbyists might find useful, so he contracted with a company to publish it. Programs like this sell for $15 to $25; the designer is paid a royalty of 40 percent of sales.

In Berkeley, where 30 percent of the adult population has some experience with computers, three hobbyist computer stores compete for customers.

A computer programmer from North Dakota worked her way around the world as an itinerant computer programmer. She was welcome to work even in countries with the most re-strictive laws about hiring foreigners.

TO FIND OUT MORE:

The Datasearch Guide to Low Capital, Startup Computer Businesses (Datasearch Inc., 730 Waukegan Rd., Suite 108, Deerfield, IL 60015) has 21 low-capital opportunities to present as well as a short crash course on selling to the computer industry. Excellent ideas.

═══════ 132 ═══════
WRITE A HOW-TO BOOK

From cookbooks to plant-growing books to sex books, how-to's are the best-selling books in America today. And you can earn a living writing them.

Both authors of this book have written other how-to's. Rosenthal is the co-author of the *Marijuana Grower's Guide* (And/Or Press). Lichty is the author of *The Do-It-Yourself Guide to Alternative Publishing* (Alternative Press Syndicate). Those two books and this one all took considerable research but are, in our opinions, well worth the time and effort.

You don't have to be a Faulkner or Hemingway to write a how-to book. If you are, all the better. You do have to have expertise in an area about which people want to learn. You may have that expertise already or you may get it through research—interviewing experts, visiting the library, experimenting, whatever.

The hardest job for a beginning writer is to find a publisher. The big publishing houses in New York are obvious—but there are also thousands of smaller publishers around the country who may be interested. Bookpeople, a small press distributor in San Francisco, currently distributes books from over 450 publishers, so your possibilities are nearly limitless. Don't get discouraged if your book is rejected the first time around—keep in mind that the *Marijuana Grower's Guide* (And/Or Press, Berkeley, CA), which has over 300,000 copies in print, took over two years to get accepted for publication.

To secure a publisher, you'll probably need to send its editors several sample chapters, along with an outline of the book, its purpose, and how and why it will sell. Sometimes beginning authors find a better reception when they present a finished manuscript. Make arrangements with the publisher (a signed agreement) on the advance and royalties. Royalties vary between 4 and 15 percent of the retail price of each book sold. At a 10 percent royalty, for example, each $2 (retail) book sold nets the author 20¢.

The advance you may get is against royalties: If the publisher expects the book to sell at least 1000 copies, you may be offered a $200 advance on that $2 book at 10 percent royalties. The advance is intended to provide you with grocery money while you finish the book. You receive no royalties until those first 1000 copies of the book are sold. Then royalty payments are generally made on a quarterly basis.

Since publishing a book is a risky business (editing, typesetting, printing, binding, and distribution all cost money), some small publishers pay no advances, but offer slightly higher royalties instead.

If you can't find a commercial publisher, a nonprofit organization may be the answer. *The Do-It-Yourself Guide to Alternative Publishing*, for example, was published by the Alternative Press Syndicate, an association of alternative newspapers. An association of sailing enthusiasts, on the other hand, might publish books on how to sail (from the tiniest sailboat to the largest yacht), how to sail safely, how to build a sailboat (with plans for different sizes and types of sailboats), how to buy a sailboat (a consumer guide), how to care for a sailboat, how to win sailboat races, etc.

You may decide to publish it yourself. This does not mean hiring a vanity (subsidy) publisher, whom you pay to publish your book, and who then charges you for any copies you might want and does very little distribution for the most part, despite claims to the contrary.

Instead, have a printer do the job. You will be charged for printing and binding. Sometimes printers also typeset; or you can rent an IBM Composer or Selectric and set your own type. You can also have it done by a typesetting company. Then the books are yours. Do your own distribution, or have a company or organization advertise and distribute it. Go back to that sailing association with a distribution offer. Small publishers' book distributors (like Bookpeople) may offer to sell the book to retailers.

Whatever method you choose, how-to book writing is not difficult. Carla Emery in Kendrick, Idaho, for example, sold 20,000 copies of the *Old Fashioned Recipe Book* at $12.95. Initial purchasers received the book chapter by chapter over four years until they had over 600 loose mimeographed pages. With the last chapter came three pieces of eight-inch wire for binding. The book still has a do-it-yourself binding.

Patrick Royce of Newport Beach, California, has been self-publishing *Royce's Sailing Illustrated* since 1956. His office is in his home, on his sailboat, on the beach or docks. Income is good enough these days for him and his wife to work full-time (they choose their own hours), live near the ocean, and sail all they please.

John Muir, author-publisher of *How to Keep Your VW Alive*, has sold over 500,000 copies of his book at $6.50 each.

OTHER IDEAS:

Write the great American novel.

TO FIND OUT MORE:

How to Write a Book About Your Specialty (by Thomas F. Doyle, Jr., Creative Book Co., P.O. Box 214998, Sacramento, CA 95821, 1976) is an excellent guide for the novice writer about to embark on a how-to book project.

The Non-Fiction Book: How to Write and Sell It (by Paul R. Reynolds, William Morrow and Co., 1970) is a fine book of advice for the writer of how-to's as well as the writer of other types of nonfiction.

The Self-Publishing Writer (P.O. Box 24, San Francisco, CA 94101) is a must for self-publishers and also for book producers. If you decide to be involved in publishing, check this periodical out. Story after story, first-person, from self-publishers themselves, it charts both successes and failures.

PART VIII
FOR MORE INFORMATION

FOR MORE INFORMATION

ACCESS

Alternate Celebrations Catalogue (701 North Eugene St., Greensboro, NC 27401, 1975) is self-published and successful and promotes gift-making, crafts, people and earth groups, and alternate lifestyles.

Co-Evolution Quarterly (Box 428, Sausalito, CA 94965) is the *Whole Earth Catalog* on a quarterly basis, plus articles on a wide variety of subjects.

How to Live in the New America (by William Kaysing, Prentice-Hall, 1972). Says Kaysing, "We believe that the only life worth living will be in the rural areas . . . that will be the New America." His book offers know-how—on rural incomes, barter, insurance, food, housing, etc.—and shows how and encourages you to live royally on nearly nothing. A veritable storehouse of information.

The Mother Earth News (bimonthly; P.O. Box 70, Hendersonville, NC 28739) offers ideas, inspirations, hints for the back-to-the-land people, suggestions for cottage crafts and industries, and contacts with others. Emphasis on alternative lifestyles, ecology, doing more with less.

The Survivor (by Kurt Saxon, Atlan Formularies, P.O. Box 438, Eureka, CA 95501) is filled with such useful information as how to make a houseboat (from 1919 *Popular Mechanics*), a minnow trap, a hang glider, a lathe, a windmill from scraps, and a bicycle sidecar.

Whole Earth Epilog: Access to Tools (POINT/Penguin Books, 1974) will give you more ideas than you can think about and will provide you with more resources than you could use in a lifetime. Reading it is a trip. Also get *The (Updated) Last Whole Earth Catalog*, (1975).

ALTERNATIVES

What Color Is Your Parachute?: A Practical Manual for Job Hunters and Career-Changers (by Richard Nelson Bolles, Ten Speed Press, Box 4310, Berkeley, CA 94704, 1975) is job-oriented, but one of the few which point readers in directions which make them happy. Bolles is not interested in "drudgery" definitions of work either. His book is excellent. It will make you rethink your goals and aspirations.

How to Spend More, Owe Less and Live Better (by Gloss Edwards and Virginia Biddle, Pyramid Books, 1963) compares the reader to a corporation and urges all to invest themselves wisely.

The Universal Traveler: A Soft-Systems Guide to Creativity, Problem-Solving and the Process of Reaching Goals (by Don Koberg and Jim Bagnall, William Kaufmann, Inc., One First St., Los Altos, CA 94022, 1976) is a real turn-on for your mind and your creative thinking patterns. It offers a new look at systems for problem-solving and for developing and implementing creativity.

Alternatives to College (by Miriam Hecht and Lillian Traub, Macmillan, 1974) points out, "students are channeled into college as if alternatives did not exist." It suggests ways to get to know yourself and your abilities, skills and values. Its attitudes are sometimes a little straitlaced, but it does what it says, offering helpful alternatives to college.

BUSINESS OPERATIONS

Boardroom Reports (500 Fifth Ave., New York, NY 10036) is actually intended for executives, but its timely advice and ideas from industry experts, business innovators, lawmakers and editors may open doors to fresh thinking for all in business. It does a great deal of digesting of new books and materials, and covers business planning, selling, management, investments, accounting and more.

Briarpatch Review: A Journal of Right Livelihood and Simple Living (330 Ellis St., San Francisco, CA 94102) is a journal of the Briarpatch Network, a group of people interested in simple living, openness, sharing, and learning how the world works through business. All members keep their financial records open to all, which they hope will lead to trust, responsibility, new ideas and greater awareness, as well as community and learning, two other Briarpatch values (the *Whole Earth Catalog* was the first Briar business to open its books, publishing a financial statement in each issue). Members meet to share and learn. Right livelihood implies that work should give a sense of excitement, fun and joy; room to grow and learn; challenges; and community service. The Briarpatch is a means for small, alternative businesses to help each other make it, with sharing as an alternative to greed. *Briarpatch Review* translates philosophy and practical application and business notes into print. Buy a copy and decide for yourself if right livelihood is what you believe in, too.

Handbook of Modern Marketing (ed. by Victor P. Buell, McGraw-Hill, 1970) is hundreds of pages designed as a text for the marketing executive. It teaches the principles but leaves out specifics: it is about marketing, which it teaches well, but is *not* how-to.

"Checklist for Going into Business" (Small Marketers Aid #71, Small Business Administration, Supt. of Documents, U.S. Government Printing Office, Washington, DC 20402) is a 12-page pamphlet of helpful questions and worksheets.

Marketing Success: How to Achieve It (by Louis Cheskin,

Cahners Books, 89 Franklin St., Boston, MA 02110, 1972) offers some valuable pointers on marketing, packaging and testing new products.

Business Information Sources (by Lorna M. Daniells, University of California Press, 1976) is a sourcebook for finding business facts, resources, information, statistics and trends. Well done.

The Pure Joy of Making More Money (by Donald M. Dible, The Entrepreneur Press, Mission Station, Drawer 2759V, Santa Clara, CA 95051) is solid information, from how to conduct a low-cost marketing survey for your product, writing the business plan and investment mini-proposal, finding new products and services, and financing, to distribution, sales, approaching prospects, making the presentation, closing the sale, overcoming the fear of failure, and more. This book is practical, solid, and *very* valuable.

How to Start and Manage Your Own Business (by Gardiner G. Greene, Mentor/NAL, 1975) is oriented toward traditional types of businesses and industries, yet offers some good tips and suggestions for us all.

International Entrepreneurs' (formerly *Insider's Report*; 631 Wilshire Blvd., Santa Monica, CA 90401) specializes in indepth reports (three in a typical issue) on small business opportunities. Generally, the ideas covered are the latest trends in small business—a profitable free-style university, cookie shop, day-care center or newsletter, for example. Reports from the magazine are later offered individually, usually for $10 to $15— they're not long, but they're a fairly complete guide; write for a list. The preliminary start-up details common to all business ventures can be found in Special Report #500.

The Journal of Small Business Management (quarterly) is published by the National Council for Small Business Management Development (University of Wisconsin—Extension, 929 N. 6 St., Milwaukee, WI 53203). There's a good "how-to" to be found here. Council members regularly conduct, sponsor or attend classes, programs or seminars that deal with aspects of small business management. The council also holds annual conferences.

Small-Time Operator: How to Start Your Own Small Business, Keep Your Books, Pay Your Taxes, and Stay Out of Trouble! (by Bernard Kamoroff, C.P.A., Bell Springs Publishing, P.O. Box 322, Laytonville, CA 95454) includes all the ledgers and worksheets you will need for a year. It's probably the most commonsense book on developing businesses yet written. Once you decide how you will earn a living without working for someone else, get a copy!

Accounting for Everyday Profit (by the J. K. Lasser Tax Institute, Cornerstone Library Publications, 1971) explains the use of accounting, what statements show and how they provide guides to the most profitable actions, how to keep and use forms and records, how to budget and plan taxes and investments. You need to know accounting basics to use this book.

How to Form Your Own Corporation (by attorney Anthony Mancuso, Nolo Press, Berkeley, CA) is a complete guide should you decide to incorporate. It's written to save you the cost of a lawyer while making the process less intimidating. Another book in the genre is *How to Form Your Own Corporation Without a Lawyer for Under $50* (by Ted Nicholas, Enterprise Publishing Co., 1300 Market, Wilmington, DE 19801).

National Small Business Association (Jefferson Bldg., 1225 19 St., N.W., Washington, DC 20036) provides no information on starting new businesses. It does represent the small business community in Washington. Among its newsletters are *The Voice of Small Business* and *Action Bulletin*. Also offered is a service to notify you whenever the government is asking for bids on the product or service you sell, giving you a chance at a governmental customer.

The Small Business Administration (SBA) (U.S. Dept of Labor, Washington, DC 20416) is well worth checking out. It holds free workshops at least once a month in 90 U.S. cities. It sponsors SCORE, the Service Corps of Retired Executives (national office: 1441 L St., N.W., Washington, DC 20416), which sends out retired executives to consult with new small business ventures at no charge. It sponsors the Active Corps of Executives, which makes free counseling available in many cities. Its publications include "Handcrafts and Home Businesses" (Pamphlet No. 1), "Discover and Use Your Public Library" (you'd be surprised what a treasure trove of information it is), and "Basic Library Reference Sources" for small businesspeople. The SBA also publishes scores of booklets on individual businesses and how to get started in them, as well as a "Checklist for Going into Business." Publications are available by mail from the national office or by mail or in person from local and regional offices. Other public agencies which may provide help include the Department of Commerce and metropolitan libraries devoted solely to business and government.

Small Business Reporter is a publication of the Bank of America (Dept. 3120, P.O. Box 37000, San Francisco, CA 94137) (free at all B of A branches; $1 per copy for back issues by mail; full catalog free). Business operations titles include "Understanding Financial Statements," "Marketing New Product Ideas," "Steps to Starting a Business," "Financing Small Business" and "Advertising Small Business." Business profiles are available on handcraft businesses, bookstores, health-food stores, mail order, hairgrooming salons, property management, and many more. A profile of the equipment-rental business, for example, discusses types of rental operations, getting started, the market, locations, licenses, permits and taxes, investment, financing (noting "many lenders will expect the prospective rental man to be sufficiently adept . . . to do his own repair work in the beginning"), insurance, suppliers, equipment purchases, maintenance, replacement, depreciation, rates, agreements, deposits, employees, advertising and promotion, and security—in 18 pages. Thorough.

Running Your Own Business (by Howard H. Stern, Ward

Ritchie Press, Pasadena, CA, 1976) is a good primer on starting
and running a business. It can be helpful.

Successful Direct Marketing Methods (by Bob Stone, Crain
Books, 740 Rush St., Chicago, IL 60611, 1975) teaches marketing and advertising techniques and applications (mostly mail)
with facts, figures, and case histories.

IDEAS

Free Enterprise (formerly *Capitalist Reporter*; by subscription
only; 800 Second Ave., New York, NY 10017) is filled with
small business tips and ideas, as well as ideas for living better on
less. It's a good magazine.

The Teenage Employment Guide (by Allan B. Goldenthal,
Regents Publishing/Simon & Schuster, 1969) is a useful book
in counseling young people. It includes job, apprenticeship and
business ideas as well as a section on applying for jobs.

How Kids Can Earn Cash (by Mildred B. Grenier, Frederick
Fell, Inc., 386 Park Ave. S., New York, NY 10016, 1970) is
a great guide for helping kids develop business ideas.

Job Ideas for Today's Woman (by Ruth Lembeck, Prentice-
Hall, 1974) is a real idea book. Whether looking for job
ideas for yourself or someone else, you will find this book very
valuable. It is, itself, a job consultant. It has more information,
advice and direction packed into its pages than any other book
of its genre.

Spare-Time Fortune Guide (by Duane G. Newcomb, Parker
Publishing Co., West Nyack, NY, 1976) is oriented toward
money, not happiness. It's one of the orientation books: Decide
how much money you want, re-orient yourself to riches, and
you'll get them.

Organic Gardening and Farming (Rodale Press, 33 E. Minor
St., Emmaus, PA 18049) will keep you informed not only about
gardening but also about living, eating, and working near the
soil.

How to Earn a Living in the Country (Without Farming) (by William Osgood, Garden Way Publishing, 1974) is a manual for transitioning from city to country workstyles.

Spare Time: Money Making Opportunities (5810 W. Oklahoma Ave., Milwaukee, WI 53219) is as worthwhile for its ads (many for products and services you can sell) as for its optimistic informative articles.

LIVING SIMPLY

Living Poor with Style (by Ernest Callenbach, Bantam, 1972) can be helpful in finding ways to live better with less. It covers the basics (food, housing, transportation) as well as fun and games.

Doing More with Less (6595 Heatherheath, West Bloomfield, MI 48033) is a little magazine on living lightly. Articles cover weatherizing, recycling, a whole-wheat quiche recipe, and more. Nice.

How to Live Rich When You're Not (by Rebecca Greer, Ballantine, 1975) is one of the better books of this genre. It covers three times the territory most of these do, applies to those earning incomes ranging from meager to quite a lot, and is authoritative.

How to Live Cheap but Good (by Martin Poriss, Dell, 1975) points out that "You don't have to be rich in dollars and cents—only in common sense and imagination—to live the way you want to." It covers the basics plus furnishings and home repairs.

Rain Magazine (2270 N.W. Irving, Portland, OR 97210) is a little magazine with big news. It provides access to information of an ecological or alternative nature. It's heavy on alternative technology. Several RAIN people have participated on various boards and panels, including ones which advise "new age" inventors, Congress, and the National Science Foundation. RAIN has also published a book called *RAINbook* (Schocken Books,

1977), available in bookstores or directly from RAIN) which combines source lists, methods, projects and ideas on alternative technologies, including health self-care, transportation, shelter, agriculture, etc.

PROMOTION

Advertising Age (740 N. Rush St., Chicago, IL 60611) has reported marketing and advertising news since 1930. It covers direct mail and mail order, television, promotion, packaging, and product news, and is guaranteed to stimulate your own marketing and advertising creativity.

Art Direction and its sibling publication *Advertising Techniques* are Advertising Trade Publications Inc.'s news and techniques magazines (19 W. 44 St., New York, NY 10036). In a recent issue, for example, *Art Direction* excerpted TV cuts and magazine ads, covered trends in advertising and packaging, reported a great deal of news, and showcased the works of an upcoming photographer and an upcoming illustrator.

Printing It (by Clifford Burk, Wingbow Press, 1972) has become a classic—a hip text for learning the arts of design, layout, printing and binding.

How to Be Heard: Making the Media Work for You (by Ted Klein and Fred Danzig, Macmillan, 1974) was written to teach nonprofit groups how to use media effectively. Klein runs a communications consulting firm and Danzig edits *Advertising Age*.

Establish Yourself as an Authority (by Sol H. Marshall, Creative Book Co., P.O. Box 214998, Sacramento, CA 95821) describes methods of publicizing yourself and your abilities by first establishing yourself as a specialist, and then writing a book on the subject. Useful.

Paste-Up (by Rod van Uchelen, Van Nostrand Reinhold Co., 1976) is a basic book for layout production, emphasizing simple tools and skills.

FURTHER RESEARCH

The Creative Black Book (Friendly Publications, Inc., 80 Irving Place, New York, NY 10003) provides national free listings to: Art Supplies and Equipment; Photo, Film, A-V, Tape Equipment; Color; Illustration, Design, Creative Services; Models, Talent, Props; Photographs (original and stock); Paper; Printers; Retouching; Film Editing and Effects; TV Music and Sound; TV Productions and Animation; Ad Agencies, Employment Agencies, Schools, Organizations, Unions. Judge for yourself whether it's valuable to read, have, or be listed in.

Thomas Register of Manufacturers (see your library) can tell you where to find the manufacturer of almost any product, from stock costume watches to copper tubing to film canisters to forklifts.

Finding Facts Fast: How to Find Out What You Want to Know Immediately (by Alden Todd, William Morrow and Co., 1974) is great. Alvin Toffler says, "The shortest path between two facts may well be Alden Todd." If you do any research at all, this book is a must; it will teach you to do your research efficiently and effectively.